We Are Baptists

We Are Baptists

STUDIES FOR
OLDER ELEMENTARY CHILDREN

JEFFREY D. JONES

Judson Press ■ **Valley Forge**

We Are Baptists: Studies for Older Elementary Children

Unless otherwise indicated Bible quotations in this volume are from the New Revised
Standard Version of the Bible, copyright © 1989 by the Division of Christian Educa-
tion of the National Council of the Churches of Christ in the United States of America.
Used by permission. All rights reserved. Bible quotations designated CEV are from the
Contemporary English Version, © 1991, 1995 American Bible Society. Used by permis-
sion. Bible quotations designated TEV are from the Good News Bible: Today's English
Version. Copyright © American Bible Society, 1966, 1971, 1992. Used by permission.

The writer wishes to acknowledge the work of Ron Arena for the sessions "The Bible"
and "The Priesthood of Believers."

Library of Congress Cataloging-in-Publication Data

Jones, Jeffrey D.
    We are Baptists : studies for older elementary children / Jeffrey D. Jones.
         p.   cm.
    Includes bibliographical references.
    ISBN 0-8170-1342-3 (pbk. : alk. paper)
    1. Baptists—Education. 2. Christian education of children. I. Title.
    BX6225.J68   2000
    268'.432—dc21   00-037089

Contents

Ways to Use This Curriculum

We Are Baptists is a flexible curriculum. One way it can be used is for a six-week program to establish a foundational understanding of what it means to be Baptist. For a shorter, focused study, use the first six lessons: Soul Freedom, Believers' Baptism, The Bible, Priesthood of All Believers, Religious Liberty, and Autonomy of the Local Church. For a more in-depth study, use all fourteen sessions for an entire quarter on what it means to be Baptist. Still other ways to use these materials, especially if they are coupled with the other age group volumes in this series, include:

- Sunday church school
- a church-wide celebration of Baptist heritage
- a weekly family night program or other special gatherings for children and youth
- a Baptist heritage retreat

However you choose to use these lessons, they are designed for congregations wishing to learn more about Baptist identity and beliefs. Each session addresses a single theme, which is biblically rooted, as a way of helping to define who Baptists are and what they believe and do. Through using this curriculum leaders and learners will grow in their understanding of the denomination's heritage and the contributions Baptists have made and continue to make in today's world.

Preparing for each session is an important part of the teaching process. Become familiar with the session objectives and outline prior to each lesson. Since you know the children with whom you are working, you can decide how to adapt the material to fit their needs and interests. Less lecture and more involvement in the learning process usually works best. Be creative!

A few sessions require special materials; however, the following materials are needed for each session:

- Bibles
- a copy of the lesson handout for each child
- pens or pencils
- newsprint and markers or chalkboard and chalk

CHAPTER 1

Soul Freedom
I DECIDE ABOUT JESUS

Background for the Leader

Soul freedom. To our ears those words may sound odd. Yet they lie at the very heart of what makes us Baptists. Our belief in believers' baptism, in religious liberty, in the priesthood of believers—all the fundamental Baptist emphases—rest on the foundation of soul freedom. Simply put, it is the right and responsibility of each person to stand before God and make decisions about his or her relationship with God. Only when one has done this can the commitment of believers' baptism be made. Thus, religious liberty is essential. And living in this freedom, we become priests to one another.

Rightly understood, soul freedom is not rampant individualism, although it puts great emphasis on the individual. Rather, it is placing oneself in the hands of God, sometimes through the community of faith, sometimes all alone, but always submitting to God's will. The purpose of this session is to explore this somewhat odd, sometimes unfamiliar, but always important foundational principle of our Baptist beliefs.

"Our key is this: To understand the Baptists we must see the principle called 'soul freedom.' By this we mean the deep conviction that every man or woman has both the ability and the necessity to enter into direct saving relationship to God through Christ. Baptists believe that this is a personal relationship needing no outside mediation or formation."[1] These are the words seminary and American Baptist Churches in the U.S.A. president Gene Bartlett used to introduce Baptists to those who might not know us very well. If you want to understand us, he seems to be saying, you need to understand soul freedom. As true as that is, it is also true that many Baptists would be at a loss to describe soul freedom and the way in which it has shaped our life together as a denomination.

The word *soul* is particularly difficult. Its meaning today seems limited to the religious aspect of a person. When Baptists first began to talk about soul freedom, however, soul meant much more. They understood it to mean the very core of our being, that central part of us that provides the true essence of who we are as persons. Early Baptists maintained that the core is free—not that it should be free

and not that there should be laws guaranteeing its freedom, but that it is free. God created each of us with a free soul. In this freedom individuals develop a relationship with their Creator and discover whom God intended them to be.

Soul freedom isn't license to do anything or be anybody. Rather, it is the freedom to discover and respond to God's call in one's life, the freedom to find and follow God's will and way. Baptists have always recognized that this is something no one can determine for or dictate to another. Bartlett describes two implications of soul freedom for

---

Biblical Basis
Matthew 16:13–16

Objectives
By the end of the session children will be able to:
- describe why people respond to Jesus in different ways;
- talk about their own response to Christ.

Key Bible Verse
"'Who do you say that I am?'" (Matthew 16:15)

Baptists: "Believing in freedom of soul as the essential truth of the Christian life, Baptists historically have moved on two fronts of religious experience. (1) They have resisted anything which seemed to them oppression of freedom of soul. (2) They have insisted on anything which seemed the expression of the freedom."[2] Soul freedom leads us to resist government involvement in religion so that each person is free to pray or not and in any manner he or she chooses. Soul freedom leads us to insist on congregational government so that there is no hierarchy imposing its will or its understanding of God's truth upon others.

Thus, belief in soul freedom explains our lack of reliance on creeds. It explains the diversity that exists within and among Baptist churches and denominations. Its practice in our congregational and denominational life is also what permits the Holy Spirit to work in our midst, to open new possibilities for us, to lead us into new ways of being and doing, into new ways of faithfulness.

Working all of this out in a context of differing values, divergent understandings of God's will, and different interpretations of God's Word is always difficult. There are no set answers.

Even today the attempt to do this creates intense conversations, sometimes even conflict, within Baptist churches and denominations. The principle remains, however. Soul freedom is at the very core of what it means to be a Baptist. It is a heritage we must both celebrate and protect.

Exploring the Biblical Basis

Jesus knew the end was near. His Galilean ministry of teaching and healing was drawing to a close and he was about to begin his journey to Jerusalem— and death. It was time for decisiveness, both in his own teaching and in what he asked of his disciples. He began gently. "Who do people say that I am?" He undoubtedly knew the answer, for he had heard the gossip: "He's a prophet come back to life—maybe John the Baptist, or Elijah, or Jeremiah." The disciples reported accurately. It was what they had heard too. All this was safe enough. It's always easy to talk about what others think, what others believe. But then Jesus pushed them. "Who do *you* say that I am?" he asked. Now he had gotten personal. Jesus was asking for an "I statement."

Jesus knew that all the teaching, healing, and casting out of demons he had done was worthless unless they understood that it was more than God-talk, more than making people healthy, more than battles over rules and regulations of the faith. They needed to understand that Jesus was the Messiah, the one for whom they had been waiting, and that God was intervening in human history to offer people new life in God's kingdom.

Jesus couldn't force this truth on his disciples; they had to get it on their own. Confessing him to be the Christ must be their decision, made in full freedom, for that was the only way it would really be their faith—

a faith they could commit themselves to, even to death. That was the only way. It still is.

The Gospel writers didn't know the term *soul freedom*, but they wrote about it. Despite ridicule and rejection, the woman came to Jesus to pour perfume on him and wash his feet with her hair. That is soul freedom. The rich young man turned away because he wasn't willing to do what was needed to follow Jesus. That, too, is soul freedom.

Biblical examples of soul freedom go all the way back to the first chapter of Genesis when human beings were created in God's image. It is the freedom abused in the eating of the fruit. It is the freedom lived out in the faithful obedience of Abraham and Sarah, in the suffering of Jeremiah. Each one in full freedom, freedom granted by God, stood before God and decided. Each one in full freedom said yes or no to the call of God in his or her life. That is what soul freedom is all about.

Soul freedom was at work in Peter too. Jesus asked Peter, "Who do you say that I am?" In full freedom, from the depth of his being, with his very soul, Peter replied, "You are the Messiah, the Son of the living God." Praise be to God!

As you prepare for this lesson:

Pray for each child by name. Today's session is about soul freedom, but it is also about responsibility. Older elementary children are beginning to discover the reality and importance of both of these concepts. As you think about your students this week, reflect on ways they experience both freedom and responsibility in their lives. In what ways do they experience them in their relationships with God? Pray that this session's focus on soul freedom will awaken in them a greater awareness of their own freedom to stand before God and make decisions about their relationships with Christ.

Read and reflect on the Bible passage (Matthew 16:13–16). This session's Bible passage is a familiar one. As you read it put yourself in Peter's place. Who do the children you know say that Jesus is? Think below the surface so that you consider what they are really saying, not just the words they speak. Then consider your own reply to Jesus' question, "Who do you say that I am?" Again, move beyond the words of your response to the way you live. As you do this, you become more fully aware, not only of the great freedom we have in our relationship with God, but also of the great responsibility.

Beginning

1. *Play "Who Is It?"*
(5–10 minutes)
■ Welcome the children to class.
■ Explain that you want to begin this session by playing a game called "Who Is It?"
■ Tell the children that in this game they will each say something about another person in the class. It can be any good

thing about them that they know, such as something they are wearing, something they like to do, or their favorite color or food. For example, they might say, "This person likes chocolate chip cookies. Who is it?" Then other members of the class will try to guess who the person is. The trick in this game is to name something about the person that is not known by everyone else in the class. If the class cannot guess who it is after the first clue, ask the student to give another one. Continue giving clues until the person is identified. The game can be varied by giving clues about other people that children in the class would know, such as members of the church or famous athletes or musicians.
■ After playing several rounds this way tell the students you want them to guess one more person. This time, offer characteristics that describe Jesus: helped sick people get better, taught about God's love, worked as a carpenter, was born in a stable.

Exploring

2. *Share "what would people say" stories. (10–15 minutes)*
■ Distribute handout #1.
■ Read the Key Bible Verse together.
■ Explain to the children that before looking at the Bible passage this verse comes from, you want to read a few stories about people who might be asking similar questions.
■ Read "The Boy and the Professors" and discuss the questions at the end of the story.

■ Do the same for "A Different Kind of Doctor" and "The Day the Storm Stopped." In the discussions of the stories, encourage the children to think about reactions people would have if similar events were to happen today. They may recognize the similarity to Bible stories about Jesus, but keep the focus on how people today would react. This will make it easier for the children to relate to the Bible story, which will be discussed in the next step.

3. *Read the Bible story.*
(10 minutes)
■ Ask the children to turn to Matthew 16:13–16 in their Bibles.
■ Introduce the passage by explaining that this event was toward the end of Jesus' ministry and that by this time he was well known because of his teaching and healing and other miracles.
■ Have someone in the class read the passage as the others follow along.
■ Turn to "Important Bible Words" on the handout.
■ Review the descriptions found there.
■ Ask: "Why do you think people thought Jesus was John the Baptist, Elijah, Jeremiah, or some other prophet?"
■ Explore with the students the notion that this was the only way people could explain all the wonderful things Jesus did; the only others that they had heard of who could do similar things were prophets.
■ Relate the students' thoughts to the reactions you discussed to

the events in the three stories in the previous step.

■ Ask: "Why did Jesus ask the disciples who *they* thought he was?"

■ As you discuss this question, help the children understand that in deciding about Jesus it doesn't matter what other people think; what matters is what each one of us believes about Jesus.

4. *Explore the meaning of* soul freedom. *(5 minutes)*

■ Write the words "Soul Freedom" on newsprint or the chalkboard.

■ Explain to the class that these words are a way Baptists describe what Jesus meant when he asked the disciples who they believed he was.

■ Tell the students that soul freedom is the right and responsibility of each person to decide who Jesus is and how he or she will follow Jesus.

■ Have the students look on the handout at the banner that describes soul freedom.

■ Ask if there are any questions about the meaning of this phrase. Material in "Background for the Leader" may help you respond to questions.

Responding

5. *Decide about Jesus. (10–15 minutes)*

■ Have students turn to "Who Do You Say Jesus Is?"

■ Explain that several possible answers to that question are listed.

■ Ask students to take a few minutes to read over the list, check the ones they would use to answer the question, and add other ones if they would like to do so.

■ After allowing time for this, discuss the responses the children checked and their reasons for choosing them.

■ Ask the children to review their lists and check the one response they think is the best or most important.

■ Ask the students to use the space provided to write a brief explanation of why they chose the item they did.

■ Ask those children who are willing to share their statements with the class.

■ Thank those children who shared.

■ Use words such as these to summarize this step: "Even though Jesus isn't with us in person today and doesn't ask us,

'Who do you say that I am?' in the same way he could ask his first disciples, we still need to answer this question. When Baptists talk about soul freedom, we mean that we all have a right to answer that question in our own way. We also mean that we have a responsibility to answer it. Part of what we need to do as Christians, then, is to learn as much as we can about Jesus, so that we can answer this question in the best way possible."

6. *Close with a song and a prayer. (5 minutes)*

■ Have the children help select a song they know that highlights the different names of Jesus or encourages them to make a decision about Jesus, such as "He Is Lord" or "Jesus, Name above All Names." Sing it together.

■ Close with a prayer thanking God for the freedom to decide about Jesus and asking for help as we make our decisions.

Notes

1. Gene Bartlett, *These Are the Baptists* (Royal Oak, Mich.: Cathedral Publishers, 1972), 2.
2. Ibid.

CHAPTER 2

Believers' Baptism
SAYING YES TO JESUS

Background for the Leader

In a very real sense, baptism is what makes Baptists Baptist. At least it is the characteristic about us that people first noticed and by which we got our name. We baptize in a different way and at a different time than many other Christian groups do. We baptize people when they are old enough to understand what following Jesus Christ means and when they make such a commitment. When Baptists baptize, instead of sprinkling, they immerse the person in water.

As with our other beliefs, there is strong biblical support for the way Baptists baptize. The Greek word that in the New Testament is translated "baptize" means literally "to dip under." This form of baptism is grounded in the New Testament. The time of baptism is as well. Jesus was baptized as an adult. All the New Testament stories of baptism are of people who were old enough to have experienced the saving grace of Jesus Christ in their lives, and they had made a conscious decision to accept Christ as their Lord and Savior.

We can clearly affirm a strong Baptist tradition regarding baptism. Baptism is for those who have experienced the saving power of Jesus Christ in their lives. Because their lives have been transformed by Christ, baptism is for those who are willing to commit to following in the way of Christ. This is what Baptists have affirmed since the day in 1609 when John Smyth baptized himself and a small band of believers in Holland and formed the first Baptist church.

Baptists believe in the baptism of believers. A person must be able to make a conscious decision that is based in his or her belief about Christ before asking to be baptized. Conscious commitment to Christ as Lord and Savior requires the asking and answering of important questions related to life and faith. When the individuals affirm that the answers of the gospel are the answers that will shape their lives, they may be baptized. All of this assumes a maturity that enables an individual to make both decisions and commitments.

Baptists affirm baptism as a human response to God's action. God has acted in Jesus Christ to save us. That action is an invitation to us—an invitation to faith in God, who with great love, makes the sacrifice that brings salvation to us. Baptism is our response to that invitation. God offers us forgiveness of sins; baptism is the sign that we have accepted that offer. God gives the gift of new life in Jesus Christ; baptism is the sign that we have accepted that gift. God calls us to live lives worthy of the gift we have been given; baptism is the sign that we have accepted that call.

Baptists practice baptism by immersion. The literal meaning of baptize, "to dip under" or "to submerge," coupled with strong biblical support, upholds

---

Biblical Basis
Acts 8:26–40

Objectives
By the end of the session children will be able to:
- retell the story of the baptism of the Ethiopian official, explaining what led to his baptism;
- describe what a decision to be baptized would mean for them.

Key Bible Verse
"What is to prevent me from being baptized?" (Acts 8:36).

the Baptist practice of immersion. Baptism by immersion symbolizes the dying to the old life and rising again to new life in Christ. This reflects the experience of those who seek baptism and further supports the practice of immersion.

Exploring the Biblical Basis

The eunuch was an official in the Ethiopian court in charge of the queen's finances. In the heat of the day, he traveled a wilderness road on his way home. He was a religious man, or at the very least, a man with religious sensitivity. He had been in Jerusalem for worship, seeking to experience God more fully in his life. He was possibly a convert to Judaism or a God-fearer, someone who read the Law and participated in religious ceremonies but had not been circumcised and become a Jew. As he read the Scripture, he may have asked: How does this religion fit together? What difference will it make for my life? Is this something I can commit to without hesitation?

In this story, the eunuch is trying to understand just a bit more about faith. He seeks answers for himself and his life. Perhaps that would have been all, but God intervened. An angel of the Lord appeared to Philip and commanded him to go to this road, to meet this Ethiopian, to answer his questions, to lead him further along in his journey of faith, and to baptize him in the name of Jesus Christ.

This story comes at an interesting point in the Book of Acts. Persecution in Jerusalem caused believers to escape to the countryside. Philip went to Samaria. There he shared the Good News and baptized the Samaritans who came to believe in Jesus Christ. The story of the traveling Ethiopian immediately follows this story. In chapter 10, the story of the baptism of a Gentile named Cornelius is told. In bold fashion Acts tells the story of the spread of the gospel to increasingly different people. It describes the power of the gospel to touch and transform people in unexpected ways.

Baptism is the central focus of all of these people's experiences. Their baptism confirms their faith in Jesus Christ and publicly declares their commitment to the new life they have chosen to follow. From the earliest days of the church, baptism has played and continues to play that role in the lives of believers.

As you prepare for this lesson:

Pray for each child by name.

As you prepare for this session take time to remember and offer a prayer for each of the students in your class. Offer thanks to God for the gifts that each one brings to the class. Ask God to be at work in the children's lives to help them grow in their relationship with Christ. Pray for deeper sensitivity to each one and to his or her individual gifts and needs. All of this will enable you to teach more effectively

and faithfully as you share God's special word with the children.

Read and reflect on the Bible passage (Acts 8:26–40). During the week read the primary scripture passage used in this session. While you read the story of the Ethiopian official's baptism, reflect on your own baptism and the meaning it had for you. In what ways are you continuing to grow in your ability to live out the commitment to Christ you made at that time? Consider talking about this with the children during the session. Also review the additional passages that will be used during step 4 to help children discover some of the meaning of "the good news about Jesus": Matthew 5:43–44; 7:12; 28:18–20; Mark 1:14–15; 9:33–37; Luke 4:18–19; John 3:16; 10:10; 11:25–26; 14:15; 15:12–14. These familiar passages are used in this session to help the children develop a fuller understanding of what it means to follow Jesus.

Beginning

1. *Share a story about Jamal. (5–10 minutes)*
■ Welcome the children and explain that today you will be exploring the meaning of baptism.
■ Write "Saying Yes to Jesus" on the chalkboard or newsprint.
■ Explain that when we are baptized we are saying yes to the things that Jesus asks us to be and do.
■ Distribute handout #2 and together read the story "A Big Day for Jamal."

- When you have finished, discuss the following questions with the class: Why was Jamal so excited? Why do you think baptism was such an important event in his life?
- Use material in the "Background for the Leader" section to help you explain the meaning of baptism.
- Share in simple form the three Baptist affirmations about baptism that are mentioned there and that also appear in the story: (1) baptism of believers, (2) baptism as a human response to God's action, and (3) baptism by immersion.

Exploring

2. *Read and reflect on the Bible passage. (10–15 minutes)*
- Have the children take turns reading Acts 8:24–40. As the reading progresses, stop to explain anything you think the children may not understand. Explain the identities of the following: (1) Philip, a disciple of Jesus who had been preaching in Samaria, a nearby country, and who had baptized many converts to Christianity; (2) the Ethiopian, a man from the African country of Ethiopia, who was an official in the court of the queen; 3) Isaiah, a prophet who lived several hundred years before Jesus. (Show the children the Book of Isaiah in the Old Testament, pointing out Isaiah 53:7–8, from which the Ethiopian was reading.)
- When you have finished reading the story, point out, briefly and simply, that the three Baptist

affirmations about baptism that appeared in the story about Jamal are also present here. A long discussion of these points will not be meaningful for the children.
- Ask the children to turn to "Acts 8 Crossword Puzzle" on the handout and work in pairs to complete it. The correct answers are: 1, baptized; 2, angel; 3, good news; 4, Isaiah; 5, Philip; 6, Ethiopia; 7, chariot.

3. *Prepare and present a skit. (15–20 minutes)*
- Now that the children are familiar with this Bible passage, ask them to prepare a skit that tells the story. Although there are only three characters specifically mentioned in the story, help them develop a part for everyone in the class: servants for the Ethiopian official, horses for the chariot, or even trees growing next to the water!
- Another option would be to ask the class, "If this were to happen today, what do you think the story would be like?" Then have them develop a contemporary version of the story involving people in your own community.
- After the skit is planned, have the students act it out. This can be an enjoyable experience even if you are the only member of the audience, but you may want to invite others to join you. If there is another older elementary class using this same material, the classes could present their skits to each other. Students could also share the skit with a younger elementary class or parents of the children.

Responding

4. *Explore "the good news about Jesus." (10 minutes)*
- Remind the class that the Bible tells us that while Philip was with the Ethiopian he not only explained the meaning of the passage from Isaiah, he also told him "the good news about Jesus."
- Ask them to share what they think this good news is.
- Write their suggestions on the chalkboard or newsprint so that everyone can see them.
- Ask the children to turn to "The Good News about Jesus" on the handout.
- Explain that you are going to conduct a quick investigation to discover more about this "good news" that Philip talked about.
- Have them team up in pairs and then assign a passage to each pair.
- Tell them that their task will be to read the passage and then write its meaning in their own words.
- Allow 4–5 minutes for this work and then ask the pairs to share with one another. Encourage students to write each group's statement in the space provided.
- When everyone has reported say: "We've discovered more of the good news about Jesus that Philip shared with the Ethiopian. It was this good news that the Ethiopian believed, and because he believed he wanted to be baptized. The Ethiopian shows us something very important about our faith: It's never enough just to say we believe. We need to act like we believe, too. That's what

it means to say yes to Jesus. It's saying yes to all the things Jesus taught us about living."

5. *Decide another way to say yes to Jesus. (5 minutes)*
■ Tell the children that all of you have already said yes to Jesus in some ways: "You're all here in Sunday school. Some may have been baptized already. But saying yes to Jesus is something we keep on doing each day of our lives—when we're children and when we're adults.

We grow in our relationship with God by saying yes to more of what Jesus wants us to be and do each day."
■ Ask the children to turn to "Ways of Saying Yes to Jesus" on the handout.
■ Have them check each thing they now do.
■ Invite them to add additional ways of saying yes to Jesus that they think are important.
■ Ask them to think about one or two items they didn't check that they would like to do or

one they checked that they would like to do better. Have them circle these.
■ If older elementary children are baptized in your church, you may want to take this opportunity to encourage the students to think about this special way of saying yes to Jesus.
■ Invite the children to share the items they circled.
■ Offer a prayer thanking God for the opportunity we have to keep on saying yes to Jesus and asking God for help in doing this.

CHAPTER 3

The Bible
POWER FOOD FOR THE SOUL

Background for the Leader

The Bible is important in the life of Baptists—children and adults! With the help of adult teachers, children can learn many things from the Bible. The seeds we plant in our children today will blossom as they move through their teen years and on into adulthood.

In Paul's letter, he reminds Timothy "that ever since you were a child, you have known the Holy Scriptures" (v. 15). As a teacher of older elementary children, you have a wonderful opportunity to ground your students in the Word of God. Often adults think of the Bible as an "adult book"—a book with adult themes, adult situations, and adult vocabulary. But the Bible, God's message, is powerful for children as well.

Many older elementary children love books. Their reading skills have improved dramatically since the early primary years, and they spend a fair amount of leisure time reading mysteries and adventure stories or soaking up the comics or sports books or fashion magazines. Like adults, children read to entertain themselves, to learn about people and things, and to discover the world around them. Studies show, though, that children (as well as youth and adults) don't spend much time reading the Bible. We often hear these days about "biblical illiteracy"—even among those active in our churches and Sunday schools.

By using the Bible each week in your classroom—and by encouraging children who own Bibles always to bring them to class—you help your students form habits that will last a lifetime. As Baptists, we cherish God's Word. It is a constant that guides our lives from childhood to old age.

Exploring the Biblical Basis

The apostle Paul was facing his most trying hour. He was under arrest in Rome, convicted of a crime he had not committed, waiting to be executed. The work to which he had given his life was being overcome by persecution and defections. In spite of these afflictions, Paul showed no regret for the choices he had made. He remained faithful to Christ, fully confident that his death would lead him back to his Savior.

This is the context for Paul's second letter to Timothy. Paul's work as a missionary is over, and his life is coming to an end. It is doubtful that he will see Timothy again—and he may not have another chance to write. So in four stirring chapters he offers urgent advice as a veteran missionary to a younger colleague and friend. The message: Carry on. Keep the faith. Be a steadfast soldier for Christ even if that

---

Biblical Basis
2 Timothy 3:14–17

Objectives
By the end of the session children will be able to:
- identify reasons the Bible is important in the lives of Baptists;
- state a personal commitment they each have made in response to God's gift of the Bible.

Key Bible Verse
"All Scripture is inspired by God and is useful for teaching the truth, rebuking error, correcting faults, and giving instruction for right living" (2 Timothy 3:16, TEV).

means personal suffering and persecution.

Paul also encourages Timothy to maintain his trust in God's Word. The Scriptures, Paul believes, are the sole antidote to a timid faith and corruption within the church. Paul had seen how leaders of his day had cast God's Word aside, dismissing it as a patchwork of Hebrew thought. He knew that "all scripture is inspired by God" (3:16) and that God's Word is "able to instruct you for salvation through faith in Christ Jesus" (3:15). These were powerful words written in the first century—words that are just as timely today for those who follow Christ.

As you prepare for this lesson:

Pray for each child by name. Ask that God will use you this week to plant a seed in the lives of your students, one that will someday bear much fruit and nurture within them a deep appreciation of, and commitment to, God's Word.

Read and reflect on the Bible passage (2 Timothy 3:14–17). Think about how you can help your students discover the importance of the Bible in their lives—this week and in the weeks that follow—and ask God to make it so.

Prepare newsprint. For Step 2, print the key Bible verse (with blanks, as indicated) on newsprint or a chalkboard before the class begins. You will later give clues to help the class fill in the blanks.

Special Materials

- scissors (one pair for every three students)
- yarn (about 36 inches for each student; colors may vary)

Beginning

1. *Introduce the Bible.*
(5–10 minutes)
- Ask the students to name their favorite books. Ask what it is that they like about the particular books they named.
- Make sure each student has a chance to share. Then emphasize that books are important. Books help us to learn about people, places, and things, expand our vocabularies, and use our imagination.
- Tell the children that one of the world's most famous books is the Bible. In fact, the Bible is the all-time best-selling book, with more than two billion copies sold.
- Set up this scenario: A young girl named Corita is visiting your class for the first time. She has just moved to the United States with her family. There were no Bibles in the country where she lived. In fact, she doesn't even know what the Bible is. The class's task is to tell Corita—in five minutes or less—what they know about the Bible.
- If the children have trouble getting started, prompt them by suggesting that they consider these questions:
  — Who wrote the Bible? (Lots of people, but God helped them know what to write.)
  — Who are some of the people in the Bible? (Abraham, Sarah, Noah, Moses, Ruth, Mary, Joseph, Jesus, the disciples, and so on.)
  — What is the purpose of the Bible? (To let everyone in the world know that God loves us and has a special plan for our lives.)
  — Why is it important to read the Bible? (We learn about God's love for us through Jesus, and we learn how God wants us to live our lives.)
- Compile the class's responses on newsprint or a chalkboard.
- When the students are finished, review their responses. Then ask: "Do you think this is an adequate summary of what the Bible is?"
- Conclude this step by thanking the class for its good work.

2. *Learn the key Bible verse.*
(5–10 minutes)
- Tell the children that the Bible is a special book because it does things that no other book can do.
- Then use your own words to say: "The apostle Paul was a missionary who lived in the first century. Many of his letters are in the Bible. In one of them, to his friend Timothy, Paul explained the purpose of God's Word. Let's find out what Paul said."
- Refer to the passage written out previously on newsprint or chalkboard (with blanks as indicated): "All Scripture is inspired by _ _ _ and is useful for teaching the _ _ _ _ _ , rebuking _ _ _ _ _ , correcting _ _ _ _ _ _ , and giving instruction for right _ _ _ _ _ _ " (2 Timothy 3:16).
- Then give these clues to the class to help them fill in the blanks:

- The one who created us (God)
- __ __ __ __ __ or dare (truth)
- When a fielder in baseball misses the ball, it's called an __ __ __ __ __ (error)
- I didn't do it; it isn't my __ __ __ __ __ (make plural) (faults)
- Not dying but __ __ __ __ __ __ (living)

- When all the blanks have been filled in, ask the class to read aloud in unison the Scripture passage.
- Ask: "What do you think Paul meant when he wrote that 'All Scripture is inspired by God'?" (God didn't physically write the words of the Bible, but God did speak through those who were the authors, inspiring them about what to write.)
- Summarize the key verse by saying that God inspired the Bible so that people in every generation would know right from wrong and would live in a way that is pleasing to God.

Exploring

3. *Learn about John Smyth.*
(5 minutes)
- Read or in your own words say: "John Smyth was a famous Baptist who lived in the 1600s. He was a minister, and he spent a lot of time reading the Bible. As he read the Bible, he learned about how God wanted people to live and how God wanted the church to function. One thing he discovered was that only those who believe in Jesus and want to become Christians should be baptized. This was a radical idea because at that time everyone in the church was baptized as an infant. John Smyth's beliefs led to the formation of the first Baptist church. The name 'Baptist' came from the word *baptism*. We have Baptist churches today because of John Smyth's obedience to the Bible. So from the beginning, the Bible has been important to Baptists."
- Ask the class to work together to create a cheer or a chant to honor John Smyth. Be creative! (Note: If you have a large class, break into smaller groups, with each group creating its own cheer or chant.)

4. *Read and discuss a story.*
(10 minutes)
- Distribute handout #3.
- Direct the class to turn to the story "Food for Thought."
- Invite volunteers to read the story out loud while the others follow along.
- Follow up on the story with these questions:
  - Do any of you have a favorite person or story from the Bible?
  - Who or what is it?
  - Why is that person or that story your favorite?
  - How many of you own a Bible?
  - When did you receive your Bible?
  - Was that a special occasion? Explain.

Responding

5. *Create bookmarks.*
(10 minutes)
- Refer the children to "Personalized Bookmarks" on the handout.
- Instruct them to create three bookmarks: one for a family member, one for a friend, and one for themselves. Each bookmark should be personalized.
- Distribute scissors, crayons, yarn, and colored markers or pencils.
- When the students have finished this activity, encourage them to give the two bookmarks to the intended persons and to use the third one in their own Bibles or other books that are special to them.

6. *Close in song and prayer.*
(5 minutes)
- Have the class stand and form a circle. Ask the students to echo this line back to you in unison, increasing in volume each time:

All Scripture is inspired by God!
All Scripture is inspired by God!!
All Scripture is inspired by God!!!

- Close in prayer, thanking God for the gift of the Bible and for the presence of each student in your class.

CHAPTER 4

Priesthood of All Believers

WE'RE ALL PRIESTS!

Background for the Leader

The "priesthood of all believers" is one of *the* foundational Baptist principles. Such important emphases as religious liberty and ministry of the laity are based in it. Our understanding of church governance and discipleship grows out of it.

But what is the priesthood of all believers? Quite simply it is the conviction that "every Christian is a priest before God and to the world."[1] Being a priest before God means that each one of us stands directly before God with no need for intermediaries. No one tells us what we must believe about God or how we must relate to God. Each of us receives the blessings of salvation and grace directly from God, and each of us is accountable directly to God for our life and faith. Being a priest to the world means that each of us is called by God to a ministry within the world. We are God's representatives, God's agents. As such, we bring God's love to the world.

The priesthood of all believers has particular reference to the relationship between laity and clergy in a Baptist church. It prescribes an equality before God characterized by a shared ministry between laity and ordained clergy. If there is a differentiation between laity and clergy, it is one of *role*, not importance, power, or prestige. When a church ordains a person, it is, in this sense, saying, "We see you are gifted to play a role of leadership within the church. This will be your ministry." In this manner, ordained clergy are not essentially different from the laity; they are just set apart to use particular gifts.

It is the rare older elementary child whose concept of a minister extends beyond that of his or her own pastor. Asked to name what a minister is, most will respond with answers that point to one who is, in their eyes, the leader of the church. The minister preaches the sermon, teaches about the Bible, baptizes people, visits people when they are sick, and presides at weddings and funerals.

The Baptist concept of the priesthood of all believers provides a wonderful opportunity to help older children broaden their understanding of who is a minister and what ministry is. They can begin to see themselves as ministers for God when they encourage a friend who is sad, make and send a get-well card to a neighbor who is ill, or help a younger

---

Biblical Basis
Revelation 1:4–6

Objectives
By the end of the session children will be able to:
■ define the priesthood of all believers as meaning that all Christians are ministers;
■ identify practical ways they can minister to others at home and in school during the coming week.

Key Bible Verse
"[Christ] loves us and freed us from our sins by his blood, and made us to be a kingdom of priests serving his God and Father . . ." (Revelation 1:5–6).

sibling who is being teased by other children. Your students can reflect God's love in their lives as they do these and other things, and as they talk with friends about their church and what they do there.

Jesus welcomed the little children. Our responsibility as adults is also to welcome children and to help them recognize and respond to opportunities to be ministers to others—now and as they move into their teen years and young adulthood.

Exploring the Biblical Basis

The Book of Revelation is one of the most difficult Bible books to understand because it is written in a style called apocalyptic writing, which is unfamiliar to many of us. It is difficult to grasp the book's full meaning with great certainty, yet at points it speaks directly and clearly to us about our lives as Christians. The biblical basis for this session is such a point.

Revelation is written as a letter. Our passage comes from the introduction of the letter, which gives the sender's name, the addressees, and a greeting. The letter is from John to the seven churches in Asia. The greeting offers grace and peace in the name of Jesus Christ. As part of the greeting John reminds his readers of what Jesus Christ did for all who believe. Christ loves us and freed us from our sins by his sacrificial death. Building upon the Old Testament concept of the priesthood but

expanding it to include all believers, John states that Christ made us a kingdom of priests. Here we have one of several direct New Testament references to the priesthood of all believers. (See also 1 Peter 2:5,9; Revelation 5:9–10; 20:6). William Barclay describes it this way: "[John] means that because of what Jesus Christ did, access to the presence of God is not now confined to priests in the narrowest sense of the term, but that it is open to every [person]. Every[one] is a priest. There is a priesthood of all believers. We can come boldly unto the throne of grace (Hebrews 4:16), because for us there is a new and living way into the presence of God."[2] The passage goes on to say that service is a part of our priesthood—doing the work of God, being involved in ministry.

When these two understandings of priesthood, access and service, are held together, we begin to capture a sense of what the priesthood of all believers is about. Israel was quite comfortable with the notion that access and service, priesthood, was appropriate for a select few. To say, however, that it was for *all* believers was a radically new understanding. That concept of priesthood remains central to the life and thought of Baptists.

As you prepare for this lesson:

Pray for each child by name. Ask God to use this session to speak to the children's hearts and that, through you, the

students might begin to understand that they have a ministry in Christ's church.

Read and reflect on the Bible passage (Revelation 1:4–6). Think about ways in which you have been chosen by God to minister to others. In what ways do you act as a priest of God? What is special about this passage that you would like to pass on to your students?

Special Materials

■ several blue, green, purple, and red crayons
■ poster board or newsprint for use in a collage
■ magazines with photographs of a wide variety of people (magazines will be cut)
■ scissors (one pair for every three students)
■ tape or glue

Beginning

1. *Make a collage. (15 minutes)* Tell the class that you will begin by working together to make a collage of people.
■ Post newsprint or poster board and distribute magazines, scissors, and tape or glue.
■ Instruct the children to find photos of a wide variety of people—male and female, different ages, different races, and so on. Allow about 10 minutes for them to complete the collage.
■ When they are finished, ask the class to look carefully at the people's faces in the collage.
■ Explain that the Bible tells us that people are created in the image of God. In your own

words, say something like: "The Bible also says that those of us who believe in God and are guided by Jesus' presence in our lives have been given special skills by God, regardless of our age, our skin color, or our education. We are to use these skills to show the love of God and Jesus by helping other people. What do we call someone who uses his or her God-given skills to help others? Let's find out!"

2. *Discover ways to help others. (5–10 minutes)*
- Distribute handout #4.
- Ask the class, "Have any of you ever thought of yourselves as ministers?"
- Ask a student to read aloud the introductory comments on the handout.
- Review directions for "Helping Others."
- Ask the children to be honest as they write their responses to each of the three scenarios.
- When the students are finished, invite volunteers to share their ideas. Praise the students for their good work.
- Emphasize that when we help others, we act as God's ministers.

Exploring
3. *Find out what the Bible says. (5–10 minutes)*
- Explain that the Bible teaches us more about what God expects from us.
- Explain that one of the verses that helps us this way is from the very last book of the Bible, the Book of Revelation.
- Go over the directions for the "And the Bible Says . . ." activity

on the handout. Have the children write the passage in the space given.
- When they have completed this activity, ask them to read the Bible passage in unison.
- Explain that those who belong to God have a special responsibility to God.
- Read together the sentence below the space for the Bible passage: "As one of God's own people, you have been chosen to share God's love with other people."
- Say that the story you are about to read shows how one girl was able to share God's love with a friend.

4. *Read and discuss a story. (10 minutes)*
- Turn to "Reaching Out in Love" on the handout.
- Suggest that the children follow along as you read the story out loud.
- Ask the students to write responses to the questions.
- Lead class members in a discussion of the questions they answered.

5. *Find the hidden word. (5 minutes)*
- Explain that Baptists have a special phrase they use to describe the biblical message that all Christians are ministers.
- Review directions for the "Find the Hidden Word" activity. Hand out blue, green, purple, and red crayons, enough so that each student has at least one crayon to begin coloring.
- When everyone is finished, ask if the class knows what the word *priesthood* means.

- After they have given their answers, explain that to "be a priest" is to do something good on behalf of another person. The priesthood of all believers means that all those who believe in God should show they love God by helping others.

Responding
6. *Identify ways to minister to others, and close in prayer. (5–10 minutes)*
- Ask the students to think of one person in their family. Then ask them to name one way they can help this person during the coming week. Invite responses.
- Ask the children to think of one person in their school who may be going through a hard time. What can they do to help that person during the coming week? Again, invite responses.
- Affirm the students' work.
- Gather together in a circle. Have the children each repeat one thing they can do to help another person this week.
- Have the class respond in unison each time by saying: "You are a minister of God, [person's name]. Go now and serve others!"
- Conclude by asking the class to repeat after you, "Amen! Amen!! Amen!!!"

Notes
1. Walter B. Shurden, ed., *Proclaiming the Baptist Vision: The Priesthood of All Believers* (Macon, Ga.: Smyth and Helwys, 1993), 2.
2. William Barclay, *The Revelation of John* (Philadelphia: Westminster Press, 1959), 1:44.

CHAPTER 5

Religious Liberty
FREE TO BE BAPTISTS!

Background for the Leader

They are two of our greatest legacies—the theological principle of religious liberty and the constitutional doctrine of separation of church and state. Because of Baptists, they are part of America's fabric of life. From early colonial days Baptists have worked to establish and maintain religious freedom.

Maintaining a consistent Baptist witness for freedom hasn't always been easy. Our Baptist forebears were whipped and imprisoned. Even today many advocates of this Baptist emphasis are criticized and ridiculed. When Baptists speak of religious liberty, they mean that decisions about faith and one's relationship with God are up to the individual, not the state.

Baptists believe the church can maintain its purpose and integrity best if it exists free from government interference, whether supportive or hostile. In this session we will look at a Bible passage in which the early church and its leaders deal with this issue of outside interference. We will also explore the importance of this principle in our own Baptist history. Early Baptists didn't see things in the usual way. They had different notions than most people about what it meant to be faithful and how to respond to Christ's claims on their lives. They often got into trouble with the authorities, and these experiences shaped the Baptist understanding of religious freedom. By the grace of God, Baptists forged the experiences of religious persecution into an understanding of religious freedom. Previously, those escaping from religious persecution had established a new authority that imposed its will on others. Baptists sought to provide freedom for all religious beliefs and expressions.

Baptists have been present whenever religious freedom has been talked about. Roger Williams, although a Baptist for only a few months, was instrumental in establishing Rhode Island as a place of religious freedom and in making Baptists acutely aware of the need for this freedom. Isaac Backus, a Massachusetts Baptist pastor, was a tireless proponent of this same freedom before the Continental Congress. John Leland, a Virginia Baptist pastor, played a vitally important role in the effort to secure a Bill of Rights that guaranteed religious freedom.

Presidents Jefferson and Madison supported the secular rationale for separation of church and state. This view maintains a "high wall of separation"; it prohibits government action from imposing religion in people's lives.

A second rationale for religious freedom is evangelical in its approach. This view is based in our historic Baptist principle of soul freedom. Soul freedom

---

Biblical Basis
Acts 5:17–32

Objectives
By the end of the session children will be able to:
- explain how the experiences of Peter and Roger Williams illustrate the importance of religious liberty;
- describe in their own words why separation of church and state is important.

Key Bible Verse
"We must obey God rather than any human authority" (Acts 5:29).

is the right and responsibility of the individual to stand before God and make decisions regarding his or her relationship with God. In this view, the purpose of separation of church and state is not to protect persons *from* religion but *for* religion. It seeks to protect both the individual Christian and the church from interference from the state that can thwart vibrant faith.

The secular view of separation, for example, objects to state-mandated prayer out of a concern that prayer not be imposed on those who don't believe in it. The evangelical view of separation objects to state-mandated prayer because it believes firmly in the value, meaning, and power of prayer and refuses to let the state determine what prayer is and when it should happen.

The Baptist view of the need for separation of church and state has placed us in the company of those who have a much more secular view of life than we do. It has opened us to attacks that we are not truly "religious" or that we do not care about faith. But Baptists take faith very seriously. Baptists are suspicious of any apart from the church who would attempt to define what religion is and tell us how to practice it.

While children are not ready to understand the full importance of a principle such as separation of church and state, they can grasp the importance of being free to believe in and worship God. That will be the focus of this session.

Exploring the Biblical Basis

Peter and John had been in trouble before. Acts 3:1–4:31 tells the story of their arrest for preaching about Christ in the temple and healing a crippled beggar. After spending a night in jail, the two were brought before the council. Facing his accusers, Peter gave an impassioned speech about Christ and his resurrection. He claimed that it was this power that enabled them to heal the crippled man. Amazed at their boldness but fearful their message would spread, the authorities ordered them to never preach or heal in Jesus' name again. Peter and John replied, "Whether it is right in God's sight to listen to you rather than to God, you must judge; for we cannot keep from speaking about what we have seen and heard" (Acts 4:19–20). They then went home and prayed for boldness. Their prayer was answered, and the apostles returned to the temple to heal and preach.

It wasn't long before the apostles were back in jail. That story is in Acts 5:17–32. This time an angel appeared during the night to set them free. Back to the temple they went. The next morning the council assembled and commanded that the apostles be brought before them. Instead, one of the temple police reported that, even though all the doors were still locked, the prisoners were nowhere to be found. Everyone was stunned. Then more shocking news followed: the men they had jailed were preaching in the temple. Once again the apostles were brought before the council, which demanded that they explain the defiance of their orders. Peter said simply, "We must obey God rather than any human authority" (Acts 5:29).

A number of stories in Acts portray the early church establishing its identity, both as a fellowship of believers and in relationship with the outside world. A feature of these stories is the issue of authority: In what will we trust? Whom will we follow? This passage clearly affirms that no one or no thing except God will determine who we are or what we do. This stance led directly to the persecution suffered by the early church. It set Christians in direct conflict with religious and political authorities who sought to determine what others should think and do, what they should believe, and how they should worship. Written following the early days of persecution, this passage reflects a central tenet of the church's identity. It affirms the historical reality and the contemporary challenge that to be the church, to be persons and communities of faith, is to owe ultimate allegiance to God.

As you prepare for this lesson:

Pray for each child by name. Teaching is more than an intellectual exercise. It is an opportunity to enter into the lives of your students in a way that will enable them to grow in faith and relationship with God. Pray that God will help you do that in this session. As you prepare for class keep each of the class members in prayer. Pray that as they grow in their understanding of our Baptist heritage they will become stronger in their own faith.

Read and reflect on the Bible passage (Acts 5:17–32). Read the account of Peter before the council. Be especially attentive to the radical nature of his statement, "We must obey God rather than any human authority." In order to grasp the impact of what he said it might be helpful to imagine someone saying the same thing in a courtroom today. How would those in authority respond?

Acts 3:1–4:31 provides important background information on this passage. It will be helpful to you to read this in order to understand the events that led up to the incident described in Acts 5.

Recruit adults. Step 5 requires adult participation either by the children visiting an adult class or having some adults come to your classroom. Make arrangements for this before the class session begins. Brief the adults so they will understand the purpose of the exercise.

Beginning

1. *Play an "un-freedom" game. (5–10 minutes)*
- Tell the children that today you are going to talk about freedom, especially the freedom to believe in and worship God.
- Ask students to share their thoughts about what freedom is.
- Tell them that as a way to experience how important freedom they can play an "un-freedom game."
- Divide the class into two groups using an arbitrary

criterion, such as those with birthdays before and after June 30 or those who have blue eyes and those who do not. These groups will probably be different sizes.
- Tell those in the smaller of the two groups that they will be the "authorities" who can tell the others what to do. Suggest that their "orders" might include telling the other group to sit down, stand up, walk so many steps, or hop in place.
- Explain to those in the larger group that for the next several minutes they must do everything the "authorities" tell them to do.
- After allowing two to four minutes for the interaction, call time and bring the class back together for discussion.
- Ask: "How did it feel to have control over someone else? How did it feel to be controlled?"
- Use a statement such as this to introduce the main ideas of this session: "No one likes to be told what to do all the time. That's one of the reasons freedom is important. Another reason it is important is that being told what you must believe and think is just as bad as being told what you must do. Today we are going to look at two people who helped people realize how important it is to be free to make our own decisions about what we believe about God."

Exploring

2. *Prepare and share a Scripture skit. (10–15 minutes)*
- Divide the class into three groups, explaining that you want each group to prepare a skit that will tell part of a story.

- Explain that this is a story about how Peter and other leaders in the early church learned that freedom was important. Explain that they may be confused at first about their part of the story, but that as the three skits are presented they will learn the full story.
- Assign the following passages from Acts 5: vv. 12–17; vv. 17–21a; vv. 21b–29.
- Allow three to four minutes for them to prepare their skits.
- When they are ready, ask each group to present its skit to the rest of the class. You may want to set the scene for the skits by describing what had happened to Peter earlier. These events are summarized in the first paragraph of "Exploring the Biblical Basis" and can be found in Acts 3:1–4:31.
- After the skits have been presented, distribute handout #5.
- Ask the class to look at "Two Days in the Life of Peter."
- Work together to decide which events do not belong.
- Number those that do belong in the correct order. This exercise will serve as a review of the skits and help class members to understand the full story. The correct answers are:

(3) The prison guards could not find Peter and the apostles in the jail even though all the doors were still locked.
(X) Peter baptized those who said they believed in Christ.
(2) An angel freed Peter and the other apostles from jail.
(X) Peter fought with the police who came to arrest him.
(4) The temple police found Peter and the apostles and

brought them before the council.

(6) Peter told the council, "We must obey God rather than any human authority."

(1) Peter and the other apostles were arrested for preaching and healing in the temple.

(5) The council demanded that Peter and the apostles explain why they continued to teach when they had been ordered not to do this any more.

■ Have the class discuss this question: Why did Peter say he must obey God rather than any human authority? (Possible answers include: because what God wants us to do is more important than what people want us to do; because he believed no one should be able to tell him how to live out his faith.)

3. *Learn about Roger Williams. (5 minutes)*

■ Say: "Now we are going to learn about another man who believed he should obey God rather than human authority."

■ Tell the students that his name was Roger Williams, he lived in Massachusetts shortly after that colony was founded, and he was one of the very first Baptists. Direct the class to "A Pioneer for Liberty—The Story of Roger Williams" on the handout. Have class members take turns reading or read it yourself.

4. *Develop "rules for religion." (10 minutes)*

■ Remind the class that both Peter and Roger Williams had to

challenge authority that wanted to tell them what to believe and how to live out their faith.

■ Explain that because we live in a country where there is separation of church and state, human authorities cannot tell people what to believe or how to practice their faith.

■ Tell the class that you want them to imagine what it would be like if there were no separation of church and state. Set the scene by saying something such as: "Imagine that there has been increasing violence and conflict in the country. The government has decided that a good way to restore peace is by promoting religion. In order to do ensure there is no further conflict, the government will make all citizens follow the same rules about what to believe, how to worship, and ways to talk about their faith. You must develop these rules."

■ Allow about 10 minutes for the group to work on this. If they need additional help, suggest that the rules might be about when and where people can worship, what things can be included in a worship service, when and where people can pray, limits on talking about religion, and how much money people must give to the church and how it must be spent.

■ Direct the students to write the rules in the space provided for them in the handout.

5. *Gather reactions to the rules. (10–15 minutes)*

■ Tell the class that now it is time to share the rules

with the people who must follow them.

■ The best way to do this will involve another class or group. Take your class to an adult classroom at this point to share the rules, or ask several adults not otherwise involved in a class to come to your classroom.

■ Have the class share the rules. Then ask the questions that are found on the handout. They may want to take notes on the responses. If it is impossible to involve others in this step have class members discuss the questions among themselves.

Responding

6. *Close with reflection and prayer. (5 minutes)*

■ Remind the class of what you have studied today: the story of Peter, who believed he must obey God; the story of Roger Williams, who was told to leave Massachusetts because he would not accept human authority in matters of faith; the importance of separation of church and state in giving us the freedom to believe and worship without government interference.

■ Tell the class that Baptists have played a very important role in making religious liberty a reality in our country and that this is an important part of the heritage we share.

■ Close with a prayer thanking God for religious liberty and those who have made it a reality for us and asking for help in continuing to use this freedom well.

CHAPTER 6

Autonomy of the Local Church

IT'S WHAT CHURCHES DO!

Background for the Leader

For Baptists, the key to understanding the church is the local congregation because it is representative of the whole church of Jesus Christ. It is free to govern its own affairs and to decide how and with what other churches it will relate. Baptists call this freedom "congregational autonomy." Yet Baptist churches are not just isolated congregations. We have always seen the need to gather in associations to do things we cannot do alone and to seek counsel from one another. At times these two realities have created tension as we have sought to balance them appropriately amidst sometimes contentious issues. The principles remain valid, however, and it is those principles that are the focus of this session.

Congregational autonomy is, in the words of William Keucher, former president of the American Baptist Churches in the U.S.A., "the right of each congregation (1) to choose its own ministers and officers, (2) to establish its own covenant membership and discipline and

confessions, (3) to order its life in its own organizational forms with its constitution and bylaws, (4) to implement its right to belong to other denominational agencies and ecumenical church bodies, (5) to own and to control its own property and budget."[1]

More recently historian Walter Shurden has written, "Church freedom is the historic Baptist affirmation that local churches are free, under the lordship of Jesus Christ, to determine their membership and leadership, to order their worship and work, to ordain whom they perceive as gifted for ministry, male or female, and to participate in the larger Body of Christ, of whose unity and mission Baptists are proudly a part."[2] This means that every Baptist congregation is free to be the church it believes God has called it to be. And as always, with the freedom comes a great responsibility—to listen and respond to God's call in a particular time and place.

First, let's deal with the freedom. The Baptist concept of the church is grounded in the

concrete reality of the local congregation. That congregation is free to determine its corporate life and its relationships with others. We believe that this grounding brings life to the church and enables it to faithfully respond to God's call to ministry. No predetermined hierarchical system dictates to congregations. Each congregation can set its standards for membership, determine its

---

Biblical Basis
Acts 2:40–47

Objectives
By the end of the session children will be able to:
- list key activities of the church;
- describe new things God might be asking their church to do.

Key Bible Verse
"They devoted themselves to the apostles' teaching and fellowship, to the breaking of bread and prayers" (Acts 2:42).

structure and organization, choose its style of worship. There is much in common among Baptist churches in these areas, but each congregation is free to change as it understands God's will for itself.

This includes the freedom to relate to other churches through denominational and ecumenical structures. As part of these relationships, the structures may set additional criteria for membership and participation. At times there is significant debate over what those criteria should be. Once they are decided, however, each congregation retains its right to determine whether or not to continue in relationship with those structures. That freedom is the very core of congregational autonomy.

With this freedom, however, comes the great responsibility of responding to God's call so that the congregation will remain faithful in its ministry. No one can tell a local Baptist congregation what it must be and do except God. The congregation's responsibility is to listen and obey when God speaks. Thus, each local congregation needs to develop a listening stance, refusing to be so caught up in its own issues and survival that it cannot hear God's voice. It must be open to change, willing to move in new directions when God calls and willing to risk seeing and doing things differently from others in obedience to God's will. Each congregation must bear its own responsibility rather than relying on outside structures to tell it how to be faithful.

Exploring the Biblical Basis

The Bible passage for this session is the first description of a church in the New Testament. Although only a few verses, it tells us much about the nature of the church and the life of a local congregation.

The story picks up immediately following the gift of the Holy Spirit at Pentecost. Peter has preached a great sermon proclaiming the Good News of Jesus Christ. Many believe. Those who do are gathered into a community of faith that is the church.

Key Baptist principles about the church are illustrated in this passage.

The church is a community of believers (v. 41). Baptists call it "regenerate church membership." This means that only those who have experienced the saving and transforming power of Jesus Christ in their lives are ready for membership.

Baptism is the introductory rite of membership (v. 41). Those who believed were baptized and became members of the church. This is one of several biblical reference points for our belief in believer's baptism.

Learning, fellowship, worship, and prayer are essential elements of congregational life (vv. 42, 46–47). These words, while not all-inclusive, are the first that describe congregational life in the early church. They inform us about important elements of church life today.

Wondrous things happen within the fellowship of the church (v. 43). The passage

refers to them as "wonders and signs." They testify to a faith in the great things that happen when two or three are gathered together in the name of Christ.

There is a great intimacy of sharing within the congregation (vv. 44–45). The passage speaks of everyone selling their possessions and holding everything in common. While most churches do not follow that practice today, it is an appropriate image for the depth of commitment to one another that is to be found within a congregation.

As powerful as this community experience is for those who share it, there is always an openness to others, a desire to incorporate new believers whom God provides (vv. 41, 47). The power of the gospel and the love that is evident in the community attract others, and the congregation is always open to receive them.

From the New Testament perspective all of this happens within the context of the local congregation. There are no church structures and hierarchies. These words, which are used to describe the very first church, are words that shape the life and faith of local congregations.

As you prepare for this lesson:
Pray for each child by name.
Even children have opinions about the church. Each child in your class attaches some meaning to church as it is made real for him or her in your local congregation. For some, these meanings may be very positive; others

20

may have decidedly mixed feelings about the church and your congregation. As you pray for your students this week, focus on what their experience of church has been. Pray also that through the class session they may develop a clearer understanding of their freedom and responsibility to be the church together.

Read and reflect on the Bible passage (Acts 2:40–47). Use the material in "Exploring the Biblical Basis" to guide your reflection on the passage. Consider ways in which you have experienced each of the key Baptist principles in your own life and congregation. Reflect on the principles that are missing in your own life and how that might be changed. To get a full picture of the context of this passage and for the story that will be included in the session, read the story of Pentecost, which begins in Acts 2:1.

Sketch a floor plan. Use the chalkboard or newsprint to sketch a floor plan of your church to be used in Step 3. Make certain to allow space outside the floor diagram in which to list things that happen outside the church building.

Beginning

1. *Explore church.*
(5–10 minutes)
■ Welcome the children as they arrive. When all are present, tell them that today they are going to be considering all the different things that happen in church.
■ Distribute handout #6. Point out the word *church* that is written vertically.

■ Ask the children to look at each letter of the word and list words that contain it that describe something in church, something that happens in church, or something that they like about church. For example the "c" could be the first letter of the word *choir* or the fourth letter of the word *sanctuary.*
■ Allow a few minutes for the children to work individually and then ask them to share the words they chose. If you think class members will have difficulty with this, work on it together. Write the letters on the chalkboard or newsprint and lead the class through the process of finding words that fit.

Exploring

2. *Discover important things churches do. (10–15 minutes)*
■ Ask the children to turn to Acts 2:40–47 in their Bibles.
■ Use material from "Exploring the Biblical Basis" to set the scene for the passage. Be certain to include these points:
— This passage describes the time just after Jesus went back to heaven following the Resurrection and the Holy Spirit came to his disciples.
— The Holy Spirit gave those who believed in Jesus the power and ability to tell others about him.
— Those who believed in Jesus gathered together.
— This passage described what they did.
■ Read or ask someone in the class to read the passage.
■ Have the children turn to the word puzzle "Things Churches Do" on the handout.

■ Tell them that there are six things mentioned in the passage that the church did and the words can be found in the word puzzle. Explain that the other words listed on the page are not mentioned in the passage, but they are also things churches do and can be found in the word puzzle.
■ Have the class work on the activity together. Each time a person finds one of the words, he or she should call it out and tell the class where it is. When someone finds a word or phrase from the passage, have everyone write it in one of the six blank spaces. Words can be found vertically, diagonally, and horizontally.
■ When you have completed the puzzle, celebrate!
    The answers are on the following page. (The six words found in the passage are: *pray, break bread, teach, worship, baptize,* and *fellowship.*)

3. *Draw a picture of your church. (10–15 minutes)*
■ Ask the children to look at the list of words from the word puzzle.
■ Then have them place the activities in the appropriate areas on the floor plan you have sketched on the chalkboard or newsprint.
■ When you have finished placing the words, ask the children if they can think of other things the church does. Place these in the proper spaces, as well.
■ Then comment on everything that the church is doing. Note that what's really important is not just the things that are done,

Answers to Things Churches Do

```
S  P  O  H  I  U  T  R  W  Q  A  O
H  L  E  A  R  N  D  G  J  L  X  R
A  V  P  V  B  N  S  H  A  R  E  H
R  B  R  E  A  K  B  R  E  A  D  Z
E  M  A  F  P  N  V  S  Z  K  H  X
J  F  Y  U  T  E  S  T  I  F  Y  E
E  S  Q  N  I  W  R  E  Y  N  I  G
S  O  Y  P  Z  T  G  A  B  D  G  L
U  W  D  V  E  R  A  C  K  M  A  K
S  T  H  E  L  P  I  H  S  R  O  W
P  I  H  S  W  O  L  L  E  F  H  J
R  E  A  D  T  H  E  B  I  B  L  E
```

■ Review the list of words in the word puzzle, asking if these suggest something that could be done.

■ Encourage the children to dream about the new thing God wants your church to do. If they need more help with this, suggest that they focus on one item, such as care, and think about people they could care for, both in the church and in their community.

■ As the children make suggestions, list them on newsprint or the chalkboard.

■ Affirm every idea, as this isn't the time to think about practical concerns, but a time to dream.

---

but the difference they make in people's lives as they develop a deeper relationship with God and do the work that God wants them to do.

■ Celebrate all that happens in and through your church.

4. *Describe congregational autonomy. (5 minutes)*

■ Direct the children to the description of congregational autonomy that appears on the handout.

■ Tell them that this as a phrase used by Baptists to describe what they believe about the church. Baptists have decided it is the best way for churches to accomplish all the things they should do.

■ Read over the description and use material in "Background for the Leader" to explain any parts of it that the children might have difficulty understanding.

5. *Dream about the church. (10 minutes)*

■ Ask the class to turn to "Ben's Idea."

■ Introduce the story by reminding the class that congregational autonomy means that everyone in a church is responsible to think about what God wants the church to do. Explain that this story is about a person their age and about how he fulfilled that responsibility.

■ Read or have someone in the class read the story.

■ Ask the children what they think about Ben's idea. Do they think it really was a way God helped the church discover a new thing that God wanted them to do?

■ Ask the children to dream about your own church. Remind them that, just like Ben, they can help the church live up to the responsibility of doing what God wants it to do.

Responding

6. *Close with a prayer. (5 minutes)*

■ Have the children review the list you have created.

■ Ask if there is something there they would like to do. If so, help them decide how to proceed. This may be the beginning of a project for your class to take on, just as Ben's class did.

■ Close by asking for God's help in accomplishing more new things that God wants the class and church to do. Give thanks for the Baptist freedom we have that allows us to decide what our church will be and do.

Notes

1. William H. Kuecher, "Congregational Autonomy," *Baptist Leader*, March 1976, 49.
2, Walter Shurden, *The Baptist Identity: Four Fragile Freedoms* (Macon, Ga.: Smyth and Helwys, 1993), 33.

CHAPTER 7

Ministry of the Laity

I'VE GOT A GIFT TO SHARE

Background for the Leader

Ministry of the laity is part of our Baptist tradition. Yet some people believe that one of the greatest challenges facing the church today is the need to rework our understanding of ministry as something shared by both clergy and laity. This view is forcefully presented by church consultant Loren Mead in his book *Five Challenges for the Once and Future Church*.[1] Mead argues that an important part of meeting that challenge will be the development of a better understanding of the role of the laity as those who have a ministry both within the church and in the world. Our purpose in this session is to explore the ministry of the laity—its tradition and its biblical foundation—and understand more fully what it means for us. As we do this, we'll discover that this important principle impacts a great variety of issues that have to do with church governance and leadership. It has great implications for the appropriate role of clergy, influences the way we approach pastoral care within the congregation, and shapes our understanding of who does mission work and

how it is done. As you look at this issue, focus on God's call as it comes to each disciple and its impact in shaping each person's ministry.

The phrase "ministry of the laity" conjures a wide variety of images in people's minds. One view suggests that laity can and should play an active part in the church's ministry by serving on boards and committees, making budget decisions, and leading in worship. The focus of ministry is inside. It can include jobs some churches hire paid staff to do but which others leave to the laity.

A more expansive and more biblically appropriate understanding of ministry of the laity begins with the recognition that all disciples of Jesus Christ have a ministry to which they are called. For some that ministry is inside the church; for many more it is outside. The ministries to which laity are called are both within the church and in the world.

Ministry of the laity affirms the importance of participation of the laity in what are often seen as clergy responsibilities. They share in pastoral care as well as in leadership in worship. They preside at the Lord's Table,

offering prayers of thanks and blessing for the bread and cup. They respond to God's call to minister to others—children, youth, and adults, who are a part of the community of faith—in ways similar to the care extended to widows and orphans by the early church. They nurture one another in the faith and in their relationship with Christ. They become "priests" to one another.

Ministry of the laity affirms the ministry each disciple has in the world. In these various ministries we use our God-given gifts as we respond to God's call to serve others in the name

---

Biblical Basis
Ephesians 4:1–7,11–13

Objectives
By the end of the session children will be able to:
■ discuss a biblical understanding of gifts;
■ describe possible gifts that God has given them.

Key Bible Verse
"... for the work of ministry, for building up the body of Christ ..." (Ephesians 4:12).

---

of Christ. The particular nature of the ministry varies greatly. It may be within the family, in the workplace, in volunteer service, or in politics or social action. Whatever its exact form, ministry begins with a stirring in the heart, as a sense of calling from God. When we are open, the Holy Spirit directs us into a particular role, not just because we want to be there, but because we believe that this is what God intends for us to do.

This understanding of the ministry of the laity is grounded in our Baptist principle of the priesthood of all believers. That principle maintains that each person stands before God; no roles elevate some above others. All can go directly to God and have a personal relationship with God without the need for another person to intercede. In the same way, all are called by God. Each one of us is called to a ministry that uses the gifts God has given us. Each of us has both the freedom and the responsibility to exercise that ministry.

The implications for the congregation of this understanding of ministry of the laity are significant. This principle emphasizes the importance of the congregational role in helping members discover, develop, and use their gifts; implies that sensitivity to God's call is a primary concern for all Christians; and suggests that churches value their members' gifts and response to God's call to minister as laity in the church and the world!

Exploring the Biblical Basis

The New Testament offers no clear description or definition of ministry of the laity, because there was no formal separation of clergy and laity in the early church. Passages such as Ephesians 4:1–7,11–13, however, provide a solid underpinning for this historic Baptist principle. They affirm three basic concepts that continue to be important for us today: (1) Christ gave a variety of gifts; (2) these gifts are to be used to equip others for ministry; and (3) this ministry belongs to all the people of God, both clergy and laity, and takes place both inside and outside the church.

The concern of the letter to the Ephesians is nothing less than the redemption of all creation. You can't get much bigger in scope than that! In the letter's view, this is God's plan; it is also what the work of Christ was and is all about. As the body of Christ, the church continues that work. This is where the ministry of the laity comes in. The ministry of the *laos*, the people of God, is to join in the work of redemption, not just of themselves, but of all creation. This is easier said than done. After this bold affirmation in Ephesians 1, much of the rest of the letter explains how this happens through the church and in the lives of Christians.

Our focus passage in this session comes from the section of the letter that deals with the church. Prior to this, the writer acknowledges the call that comes to all Christians and encourages his readers to

remain faithful to that call (4:1). He then affirms our unity in Christ: "one Lord, one faith, one baptism, one God and Father of all, who is above all and through all and in all" (4:5). This unity, however, is not sameness, for there is variety in the church, specifically a variety of gifts. In Ephesians these gifts are seen as different roles that are played in the church: apostles, prophets, evangelists, pastors, and teachers. All these are essential if the church is to fulfill its purpose. These roles exist "to equip the saints for the work of ministry, for building up the body of Christ" (4:12). Remember, the meaning of *saints* here is broader than simply those special people who have a particularly high degree of holiness or who have enabled miracles. It is the term used to describe all who have claimed Jesus Christ as their Lord and Savior, much as we might use the term *believer* or *disciple*.

The meaning of this phrase, then, is that the various gifts exist so that disciples will be equipped to do the work of the church, for "ministry, for building up the body of Christ." These are really two sides of the same coin. Ministry and building up the body of Christ are so intimately tied together that they cannot be separated. The place and nature of this work entail a wide range of possibilities.

When the letter was written, there was no clear notion of ordination. The specific roles mentioned in the passage were for everyone, not just clergy. Any of the *laos* might be in the role of apostle, prophet, evangelist, pastor, or teacher. The key was whether or not they had the specific gifts needed to fulfill these roles. The primary focus of prophets, pastors, and teachers was most often inside the church. That of the apostles and evangelists, however, was most often outside. All of these ministries led and lead to building up the body of Christ.

As you prepare for this lesson:

Pray for each child by name. Think about the children in your class, ways they are already involved in ministry, and ways to encourage them to greater involvement. As you pray for the individual children in the class, pray that they may be more aware of their giftedness and ways in which they can participate faithfully in the work of Christ.

Read and reflect on the Bible passage (Ephesians 4:1–7, 11–13). Ephesians 4 is one of the more familiar passages among the New Testament letters. Don't let this familiarity keep you from prayerful reflection on it. If you have time, read the entire letter, which isn't very long. If this is not possible, reading chapters one through four will provide a setting for the passage used in the session.

Beginning

1. *Share things we like to do.* *(5 minutes)*
■ Welcome the children to class.

■ Tell them, "Today we will talk about things you like to do and why you like them."
■ Offer a personal illustration of something you enjoy doing and the way it enables you to use a special gift or talent.
■ Explain to the children that you are going to name several areas and that you would like them to call out things they like to do in that area. Use these areas, or any that you think will be interesting to the children in your class: sports, music, school, church.

Exploring

2. *Read about Courtney.* *(5–10 minutes)*
■ Distribute handout #7.
■ Together read the story "Courtney's Gift."
■ When you have finished reading, use these questions to guide a discussion: What is Courtney's special gift? Why do you think he didn't know it was so special? How did he discover it? How did Courtney use his gift? Do you think Courtney was helping to do God's work in the way he used his gift?

3. *Explore the idea of gifts.* *(5 minutes)*
■ Ask the children for other words that could be used in place of *gift* in the story.
■ Ask: "Why do you think the word *gift* is used instead of other words?"
■ Then ask: "If it is a gift, who gave the gift to Courtney?"
■ Use a statement such as this to summarize the discussion: "Gifts are very much like talents, abili-

ties, or skills that we have. We use the word *gift* because it reminds us that God has given it to us. That helps us to realize the best way to thank God for the gift is to use it the way God wants us to use it—in doing God's work in our church and in the world."

4. *Study the Bible passage.* *(10–15 minutes)*
■ Tell the children that you are now going to look at a passage from the Bible that talks more about gifts and the way God wants us to use them.
■ Ask them to turn to Ephesians 4. Use some of the material found in "Exploring the Biblical Basis" to explain this passage to the children. Select one or two points that you think are most important and emphasize those.
■ Note that the writer of Ephesians has been discussing God's plan and the role Jesus plays in fulfilling that plan. Explain that in this part of the letter he writes about the church and its important job in continuing the work that Jesus began.
■ Have someone read vv. 1–7.
■ Point out that this section of the passage talks about what everyone in the church has in common ("one Lord, one faith, one baptism, one God and Father of us all"). It then talks about what makes us different ("a variety of gifts").
■ Have someone read vv. 10–13.
■ Then ask: "What does this passage tell us about the way our gifts should be used?"
■ Point out the key verse (v.12), which answers the question simply: God's gifts are to be used in

ministry that builds up the church.

■ Have the children turn to "Is This Ministry?"

■ Read the items on the list, asking the children to vote on whether or not they think each one is ministry. If they strongly agree it is, they should raise both arms and wave them; if they think it probably is ministry, they should raise one hand; if they think it probably isn't ministry, they should make a thumbs down sign; if they strongly believe it isn't ministry, they should put both thumbs down and wave them back and forth.

■ Have them mark each item according to the way the class voted.

5. *Do a gifts puzzle.*
(5–10 minutes)

■ Have the children turn to the "Gifts Puzzle."

■ Explain that the passage from Ephesians mentions five of the gifts that God gives.

■ Point them out in verse 11.

■ Explain that other passages in the Bible name more gifts and there are other qualities we might call gifts that are not even listed in the Bible.

■ Say: "Some of these other gifts are included in the puzzle."

■ Go over the directions and give the children time to work.

■ Bring the group back together and review the answers. The puzzle solution is at right.

■ If the children need help, list the words on the chalkboard or newsprint: *caring, creativity,*

faith, healing, helping, joy, kindness, leading, life, singing.

6. *Decide ways to use gifts for God. (10 minutes)*

■ Explain that everyone, including each of them, has been given a gift from God that can and should be used in ministry, doing God's work.

■ Point out the lists of gifts and ministries that you have created during the class.

■ Ask: "What gift has God given you? How will you use it?"

■ Allow time for the children to think about gifts they have and how they might use them.

■ Ask the children to use the space provided on the handout to write some of their thoughts about these questions.

■ If the children need encouragement, refer to some of the gifts included in the puzzle. Ask: "Who do you think might have the gift of _____? How does he or she use that gift?"

■ Continue this process using other gifts from the puzzle.

■ Encourage the students to share what they wrote.

Responding
7. *Close with prayer.*
(5 minutes)

■ Remind the class that everyone who believes in Jesus has a ministry and that part of following Jesus is discovering our gifts and deciding how to use them.

■ Say: "This is one of the basic beliefs we share as Baptists."

■ Close with a prayer thanking God for the gifts we have been given and asking for help in using them the way God wants.

Note
1. Loren Mead, *Five Challenges for the Once and Future Church* (Bethesda, Md.: Alban Institute, 1996), 1–15.

Answers to Gifts Puzzle

26

CHAPTER 8

Discipleship
GROWING UP TO JESUS

Background for the Leader

Christians believe in discipleship—that is, they believe that all who claim faith in Jesus Christ are called to learn about and follow in the way Christ teaches. Baptists, however, bring another dimension to this common belief. Baptists believe in the priesthood of all believers. This notion, that we all have both direct access to God and a ministry from God, makes discipleship an even more important part of our life and faith. It is through discipleship that our priestly role is developed and our ministry lived out.

A disciple of Jesus Christ seeks to learn more about Jesus and to practice what is learned each day. Discipleship is about knowing Christ, having a significant relationship with him, and living the way Christ would live. Discipleship incorporates all of our life—our being, our knowing, and our doing. This call to discipleship is set against the Baptist focus on the priesthood of believers. Because God calls each one of us to a ministry, part of growing as a disciple is discovering and living out that call.

One way to understand discipleship is to think of it as three pieces of the same pie. Each slice is different, yet each one is connected to the other, and each one has pretty much the same ingredients as the other. The three pieces of the "discipleship pie" are *deepening spiritual life, equipping,* and *ministering.*

Deepening spiritual life speaks about the need for disciples to continue to grow in their personal relationship with Christ. Relationships always require work. A relationship with Christ is no different. In fact, in some ways, it may be more difficult because there is no flesh and blood person with whom we can sit down across a table and talk. What's great about this relationship is that Christ constantly seeks us out. Christ constantly loves us. Christ constantly desires to have a relationship with us. Spiritual disciplines are the ways Christians traditionally seek to grow in their relationship with Jesus. From prayer to action, from meditation to Bible study, these disciplines are all about strengthening our relationship with Christ. As our relationship with Christ is strengthened, our spiritual life is deepened.

Equipping speaks of the need to continue to acquire the knowledge and skills that make faithful living possible. For Christians a key to equipping is found in the discovery and development of our God-given gifts. These gifts are given for ministry, to live out our lives as disciples of Jesus Christ. Being equipped, then, is the ongoing process of discovering and developing our gifts. Other important aspects of equipping include acquiring both knowledge and skills. To be disciples of Jesus Christ, we need to

---

Biblical Basis
Colossians 1:27–29 and Luke 2:41–52

Objectives
By the end of the session children will be able to:
■ describe ways in which Jesus became mature in his faith;
■ determine at least one way they want to become more mature in their own faith.

Key Bible Verse
"... to bring each one into God's presence as a mature individual in union with Christ" (Colossians 1:28, TEV).

know who he is, what he teaches, and how we are to live. That knowledge comes primarily through Bible study. Living as faithful disciples may also require the use of particular skills, such as preaching, leadership, working with groups, carpentry, or cooking. The list is limitless and depends on the way in which we have been called to live out our discipleship.

Ministering speaks of the need to put faith into action. We do this when we respond to God's call to serve others in the name of Jesus Christ. The deepening spiritual life and the equipping both have a purpose—involvement in ministry as Christ's disciples. In ministering we are fulfilling our call and continuing to grow as disciples of Christ.

Exploring the Biblical Basis

Paul was in prison. Before him stood the stark reality that he might be put to death because of his work. He used this time to reflect on his life and ministry—the things he had been about and that were most important to him. The section of the Letter to the Colossians that is the Bible basis for this session comes from this part of his reflection.

In Colossians 1:24 Paul talks about his suffering. He rejoices in it because it completes the suffering of Christ. As Christ suffered for the church, so Paul suffers for the church. His imprisonment is directly related to the work of the church. That work is, in a word, discipleship.

It is bringing "each one into God's presence as a mature individual in union with Christ" (Colossians 1:28, TEV). The Greek word translated "mature" can also be translated "complete." We become mature as we complete God's intentions for us. This happens, Paul claims, through the proclamation of the "secret" that God has now revealed to everyone. The secret is this: "Christ is in you, which means that you will share the glory of God" (Colossians 1:27, TEV).

Through this indwelling Christ we become mature, and the work of discipleship is accomplished. For Paul this is an ongoing process. In his letter to the Philippians he refers to a race that is being run but is not yet completed (Philippians 3:12–14). Ephesians speaks of the time in the future when we will become "mature [people], reaching to the very height of Christ's full stature" (Ephesians 4:13, TEV). For now, however, the challenge is to keep growing as disciples.

Later in this section of Colossians Paul writes about how that happens. These verses are not included in the Bible basis for this session, but they are important to understanding the work of discipleship. "Since you have accepted Christ Jesus as Lord, live in union with him. Keep your roots deep in him, build your lives on him, and become ever stronger in your faith, as you were taught" (Colossians 2:6–7, TEV). These few words are rich in insights about discipleship.

1. Discipleship begins with our acceptance of Christ as Lord. Certainly we learn about being a disciple before then. What we learn helps us commit to Christ, but the actual process of discipleship begins once we have said yes to Christ's call and claim on our lives.

2. The central feature of discipleship is learning to live in union with Christ. This is possible because Christ already dwells in us. We fulfill that union when we recognize it and begin to order our lives around it.

3. Keeping our roots deep in Christ is what enables the first element of discipleship as described in "Background for the Leader." This is what deepening spiritual life is all about.

4. The other two elements of discipleship, equipping and ministering, are encompassed in building our lives on Christ. This includes how we live out our faith in our relationships and what we choose to do with our lives.

5. Discipleship is not just sit-down-and-listen teaching. It also includes the teaching that comes from living our lives alongside other disciples and following Jesus as the model of what it means to be truly mature.

The second passage children will look at in this session is the familiar story of Jesus in the Temple found in Luke 2:41–52. It is a story that interests children, because it is the only story in the gospels that is about Jesus as a child. In addition, children can find much to admire in the notion that even as a child Jesus could not only attract the attention of adults but also impress them with his knowledge and faith. As the story is retold in this session, children will be asked to place themselves in Jesus' situation and consider Jesus' own growth as one who does God's work.

As you prepare for this lesson:

Pray for each child by name.
Discipleship is important for everyone in your class. Some students may have already made a commitment to Christ in baptism while others may not have done so. Through this session they can all learn more about what being a disciple of Jesus Christ is all about. They can begin to see what they might do to be more like Jesus. Those who have not yet made a commitment to Christ in baptism can be encouraged to choose his way of life themselves. Focus on your students and where each one is in his or her relationship with Christ as you pray for them this week.

Read and reflect on the Bible passage (Colossians 1:27–29 and Luke 2:41–52). You may want to read the entire section the Colossians passage is taken from, Colossians 1:24–2:5. This will give you a better sense of the context in which Paul writes the words of the passage we will focus on. Also, read Colossians 2:5–6 and consider its insights into the process of discipleship. Take time to reflect on the key elements that you believe are

involved in being mature in Christ. How do you demonstrate these in your own life? What are the points at which you, personally, need to grow as a disciple of Christ? As you read the passage from Luke, put yourself in the place of a child in your class, considering how he or she might react to it and the reasons this passage is so interesting to children.

Beginning

1. *Play the "Couldn't and Can Game." (5–10 minutes)*
■ Welcome the children to class.
■ Tell them that today they will be looking at ways they have already grown and then at different ways in which they can still grow.
■ Distribute handout #8. Point out the section entitled "Couldn't and Can."
■ Divide the class into groups of two or three.
■ Explain that each group is to think of things they can do now that they couldn't do when they were three years old. Give an example, such as read or tie a shoelace. Tell them they have two minutes to write down as many things as they can.
■ When time is up have each group share its list and see which group had the most items.
■ Select one of the items and ask, "What would it be like if you still couldn't do this? How would your life be different?"
■ Discuss this with the class to underscore the importance of continuing to grow in life. Children are at different stages of development, so be sensitive to

those who may not be able to do some of the things the others can. When you select an item to discuss, be sure it is one all members of the class can do.

Exploring

2. *Discover a secret. (10–15 minutes)*
■ Ask the children to turn to "God's Secret" on the handout.
■ Tell them this passage is from one of the letters that a church leader named Paul wrote to some of the very first Christians. Use some of the material in "Exploring the Biblical Basis" to describe briefly the situation in which Paul was writing.
■ Read the passage together as it appears on the handout.
■ Stop at the end and ask, "Can anyone guess what the secret is?"
■ Share ideas, then have the children use the chart to decode the final phrase of the verse.
■ When you have decoded the verse ask, "Is that a secret? What do you think it means to say that Christ is in us?"

3. *Explore the meaning of the secret. (5–10 minutes)*
■ Say: "Maybe we can find out more about this secret by looking at the Bible passage this verse comes from."
■ Have the children turn to Colossians 1:27–29 in their Bibles.
■ Point out the phrase that says "which means that you will share in the glory of God" (in Today's English Version).
■ Tell the children that another translation (the Contemporary

English Version) translates this verse this way: "[Christ] is your hope of sharing in God's glory."

■ Say: "Paul is saying that part of what it means to be in union with Christ is to share in the glory of God."

■ Ask the children what they think God's glory is like.

■ Allow a minute or two for them to share ideas. Things they might mention include joy, excitement, peace, and happiness.

■ Say: "Let's look at another part of the verse that will help us understand a little more about what being in union with Christ means."

■ Point out the phrase, "in order to bring each one into God's presence as a mature individual in union with Christ," specifically the word *mature*.

■ Say: "One meaning of the word *mature* is to be grown up, to act like an adult. What will you be like when you are mature?"

■ Have the children share their ideas about what it means to be mature. Then say: "This passage says 'mature in Christ.' How is that different from just being mature?"

■ Allow children time to share responses.

4. *Explore ways Jesus was mature. (10 minutes)*

■ Say: "One way to look at what it means to be mature in Christ is to think about the ways Jesus acted like a mature person. Let's explore some of those now and see what we can discover."

■ Divide the class into groups of two or three.

■ Turn to "Jesus Was . . ." on the handout.

■ Assign one or two passages to each of the small groups.

■ Ask them to read the passage and decide what it says about the ways Jesus was mature.

■ Allow about 5 minutes for this work, then ask the children to share what they learned. Encourage the children to use the space provided on the handout to write notes about each of the verses.

■ When all the groups have reported, quickly review the qualities of Jesus that they named.

■ Ask, "Do you think you could be like this, too?"

■ Write the word *disciple* on newsprint or the chalkboard and direct the students' attention to the statement on the handout about who is called a disciple.

■ Tell the children that the first followers of Jesus, the first people who wanted to be like him, were called disciples.

■ Explain that this same word describes them, too, if they want to be more like Jesus.

Responding

5. *Decide ways to be more like Jesus. (10 minutes)*

■ Have the children look at all the items they listed in the previous step.

■ Ask them to select one that they would like to be, too.

■ Tell the children to turn to "More Like Jesus" on the handout and fill in the blank space with the quality they selected.

■ Then allow a few minutes for them to fill in the space after "because . . ."

■ Tell the children they can do this by writing an explanation, by drawing a picture, or by writing a poem or song. They can do anything they want as long as it will help others understand why they want to be like Jesus in the way they have chosen.

6. *Close with prayer. (5 minutes)*

■ As preparation for prayer, ask the children to share their work with the class.

■ Lead in a prayer asking God for help as we all try to become more like Jesus.

CHAPTER 9

Evangelism
I CAN SHARE JESUS WITH OTHERS

Background for the Leader

It is difficult to think about Baptists without thinking about evangelism. Before receiving believer's baptism, a person experiences the transforming power of Jesus Christ and makes a commitment to follow him. With this experience comes joy, forgiveness, liberation, and a new sense of meaning and purpose. Because these new feelings and experiences need to be talked about, there comes a desire to share. But the sharing is also a witness so that others may know this great experience too. That's what evangelism is all about. And that's why evangelism is so basic to being a Baptist.

It is often said that Baptists became a denomination because of mission. Our first national organizational structure, the American Baptist Foreign Mission Society, was formed to support the work of Adoniram and Ann Judson in Burma. The American Baptist Home Mission Society was formed to support mission efforts of people like John Mason Peck on the American frontier. When the Woman's American Baptist Home Mission Society was formed, its first missionary was Joanna P. Moore, already at work among the freed slaves of the American South. It might just as easily be said, however, that Baptists formed denominations because of evangelism, for evangelism was the primary focus of this mission work. The passion to share the Good News with others motivated the Judsons, Peck, Moore, and all those who supported them through the formation of these mission organizations. As Baptists, evangelism has been and still is basic to us.

Just as our understanding of mission has expanded from those early days, so has our understanding of evangelism. In recent years American Baptists have been guided by this definition of evangelism, which was adopted by their General Board in June 1984:

Evangelism is
the joyous witness of the People of God to the redeeming love of God
urging all to repent
and to be reconciled to God and each other
through faith in Jesus Christ who lived, died, and was raised from the dead,
so that
being made new and empowered by the Holy Spirit believers are incorporated as disciples into the church for worship, fellowship, nurture and engagement in God's mission of evangelism and liberation within society and creation,
signifying the Kingdom which is present and yet to come.

That's a pretty inclusive statement. At its core, however, is the sharing of the Good News of

Biblical Basis
Acts 3:1–16

Objectives
By the end of the session children will be able to:
- describe what makes a person an evangelist;
- name two things they will do in the coming week to be evangelists.

Key Bible Verse
"I have no money at all, but I give you what I have: in the name of Jesus Christ of Nazareth, I order you to get up and walk" (Acts 3:6, TEV).

Jesus Christ. Despite changes in approach over the years, despite differing styles, that has been and still is what evangelism is all about.

Like mission, our understanding of evangelism needs to be shaped today by the relatively new and all-important reality that the majority of the society in which we live has no ongoing relationship with a church. In the past we had a tendency to think about evangelism as something we do with "them"—people who are different from us. After all, nearly everyone who was like us was already involved in a church! That is no longer the case. This reality calls for an understanding of evangelism that moves beyond the mass event and into personal relationships. A new view of evangelism moves away from a single transforming experience to an ongoing process of being transformed. It calls for *each of us* to develop a renewed commitment to and understanding of the ways in which we are and can be evangelists.

Exploring the Biblical Basis

Peter was new at the practice we now call evangelism. After all, only a few weeks had passed since Pentecost, when he and others had been sent into the world to share the Good News of Jesus Christ. It must have been a challenge for him to respond correctly, to share appropriately, to help others see the new reality that had so shaped his own life. He might very well have dealt with all the same issues that confront us when it comes to being evangelists.

His interaction with the beggar at the temple, which is the biblical text for this session, was no exception. He was in a new situation that called for a new response. But Peter, led by the Holy Spirit, came through. He responded in a way that enabled faith. In doing so he provided us with a number of important insights about what it means to be an evangelist, insights we can apply to our own lives.

Peter understood that the gospel comes to people as a response to human need. The declared need was money. The deeper need was healing. The still deeper need was salvation. It was to the need for healing that Peter responded, even though that wasn't what the man was asking for. It is possible that the man's reason for not asking for healing was a belief that it was impossible.

Perhaps Peter recalled Jesus responding to a crippled man by saying, "Your sins are forgiven" (Mark 2:1–12). But Peter's response was not quite so bold. He chose to meet the man at a level of need that was both real and deep.

Peter understood what he could offer and what he couldn't. At least part of Peter's response to the man was based on understanding what he could provide and what he couldn't. Peter offered what he could, and with and through the power of the Holy Spirit, it was enough. Perhaps from the man's perspective it was more than enough. As we share the Good News we must remember that the gospel doesn't solve all problems the way people would like to have them solved. There are some things we can provide and other things that we must leave to God's infinite wisdom.

Peter was willing to risk in order make the Good News real. The risk for Peter came in at least two ways. First, there was the risk that healing would not come. The claim Peter made was a bold one made in faith. But every act of boldness is a risk. We risk that somehow we may have misread God's intention or misunderstood our purpose. We risk failing to do what we said we would do. In addition to the risk of failure, there was for Peter, and also for us, a second risk, the risk of consequence. The consequence for Peter, within a short period of time, was jail. There are, even in the twenty-first century, consequences when we share the Good News with others.

Peter was clear about the power behind the Good News. In conversation with those who witnessed the healing and speeches before his accusers, Peter clearly declared the source of the power that healed. It wasn't him or the act of healing itself that was important; it was the declaration of what that power was. The power of God is what makes healing possible. The power of God is the Good News. Evangelists speak and are empowered by this power.

Peter understood that all people have complete freedom to

respond or not respond to the Good News. Peter had a clear understanding of his role: it was to bring healing and to explain the source of that healing power. What the beggar, the witnesses, and his accusers did with that was not up to him. It was between them and God.

As you prepare for this lesson:

Pray for each child by name. If evangelism is viewed in the broadest sense as ministry with those who have yet to make a commitment to Christ in baptism, then ministry with most children is evangelism. Even beyond this, however, there is a sense in which we all continually need to be evangelized. We always need to hear Christ's word for us and our lives so that we can be brought into closer relationship with God. As you prepare for this session ask Christ what word it is you need to hear. Think and pray about each child in your class. Ask Christ what your evangelistic role with the children might be this week. Pray that you will receive the word that needs to be shared with each of them. Pray also that through this class they may develop a greater sense of themselves as evangelists called to share the Good News with others.

Read and reflect on the Bible passage (Acts 3:1–16). If you have time and would like to set these events in the broader context of the days following Pentecost, read Acts 2:1–4:31. Reflect on your own role as an evangelist. Is it one with which you are

comfortable? In what ways do you need to grow in that role? Your willingness to share about this with the children may increase their openness.

Beginning

1. *Share about important people. (5–10 minutes)*
■ Welcome the children to class and talk briefly with them about the past week.
■ Ask: "Who are the most important people in your life?"
■ Allow time for responses.
■ Ask someone to tell the rest of the group something about one of the people he or she named as important and why.
■ Encourage several children to do this. You might want to share about a person who is important to you in this same way.

2. *Introduce evangelism. (10 minutes)*
■ Explain to the children that the session today is all about sharing about someone who is very important in all our lives.
■ Distribute handout #9.
■ Ask students to follow along as you read "Mary the Evangelist."
■ When you have finished, ask what made Mary an evangelist.
■ Discuss suggestions the children make.
■ Write "An evangelist is a person who shares Jesus with others" on newsprint or the chalkboard.
■ Ask the children in what ways Mary shared Jesus with others.
■ Explore ways she shared Jesus by what she said and did. List these on the newsprint or chalkboard.

Exploring

3. *Read a Bible story. (5 minutes)*
■ The word puzzle the children will do in Step 4 is based on Today's English Version (the Good News Bible), so use that translation if possible.
■ Have the class turn to Acts 3:1–16.
■ Explain that this is a story about evangelism.
■ Ask the children to look for the things the people in the story do to share Jesus with others.
■ Read the story yourself or ask several children to read parts of it.

4. *Fill in a word puzzle. (5–10 minutes)*
■ Complete the word puzzle as a way to review the content of the story.
■ Ask the children the two questions that appear in the handout: "Who are the evangelists in this story? What did they do that made them evangelists?" Much of the sharing of Jesus is done by Peter and John, but ask the children to think also about ways in which the man who is healed shared Jesus, too. These are the correct answers to the word puzzle with the verse in which they appear: temple (1), every day (2), walk (6), John (3), gate (2), Peter (3), lame (2), surprised (10), strong (7), jumping (8).

5. *Create and share evangelism skits. (10–15 minutes)*
■ Divide the class into groups of two or three children, or more if you have a large class. If you have a small class, have all the children work together on several of the skits.

- Read the incidents that are described in "What Would an Evangelist Do?"
- Ask each group to select one incident and develop a skit that shows first what someone who is sharing Jesus *wouldn't* do, and then what he or she *would* do.
- Allow about five minutes for the groups to develop the skits, then bring the class back together and ask the groups to perform their skits for the others.

6. *Complete a personal evangelist checklist.*
(5 minutes)
- Read the instructions for "My Evangelism Checklist" on the handout.
- After allowing a few minutes for children to complete the checklist, invite them to share the items that they are going to try to do this coming week.
- Encourage them to remember these things each day.
- Suggest that they pray about doing this each morning and evening during the week.

Responding

7. *Close with prayer.*
(5 minutes)
- Close with a prayer asking God's blessing on the children in the coming week as they try to be evangelists by sharing Jesus with others.
- Include in the prayer the specific items that the children plan to do, so they can sense the support that comes to them through prayer.

CHAPTER 10

Worship
GOING TO A PARTY

Background for the Leader

Ideas about worship abound! There may be as many "Baptist" styles of worship as there are Baptist churches! With no prayer book to guide us, no book of order to govern us, each congregation makes its own decisions about worship. Everything from liturgical formality to charismatic spontaneity happens in Baptist churches. And sometimes both happen in the same Baptist church!

With so many possibilities before us, there is bound to be a healthy disagreement about what is best. There are also, from time to time at least, bound to be outright battles over what happens in the worship service. Even whether or not to sing "Amen" at the end of hymns can be a bone of contention! These disagreements testify to the important role worship plays in our lives. It truly is sacred.

If worship is sacred, it is also in many ways personal. At least that's the way people often approach it. The question many use to evaluate worship is simply, "Was it meaningful to me?" Personal meaning is important, of course, but it is not the whole story. Worship is a corporate experience, something for the people of God gathered together as a community of faith. The "we" of worship is just as important, if not more important, than the "me" of worship. The focus of worship is God, so rather than "What did I get out of it?" a more appropriate question to ask might be "What did God get out of it?" That question is certainly more difficult to answer, but asking it can, at the very least, help us keep the focus of worship in the right place.

Recent studies of worship and the role it plays in our lives reveal some interesting information. In most churches there seems to be a generational difference in what is seen as "good" worship. One study captured this difference in two simple words. Those born prior to World War II think of worship primarily as *meditation*. Those born following that war think of it primarily as *celebration*. Both are important to worship, but a view of what is *most* important shapes attitudes on a whole array of worship issues. If worship is primarily meditation, a quiet time for personal preparation before worship is essential. But if it is primarily celebration, a joyous time of community sharing makes sense. If worship is meditation, children can be a disruption. But if it is celebration, children help set the proper tone. If worship is meditation, a sermon that prompts personal contemplation is just right. But if it is celebration, that same sermon can destroy the essential mood. If worship is meditation, prayers of confession play a central role. But if it is celebration, prayers of thanksgiving are most important.

Despite significant personal differences and great differences in worship practices among

Baptist churches, there are several important common affirmations we can make. Each of these is related to the heritage we share as Baptists.

1. The differences that exist among us result from one of our most basic principles—the autonomy of the local congregation. This is why there is no prayer book, no prescribed form of worship for all to follow.

2. The centrality of the Bible in our life and faith is another Baptist principle that shapes our worship. The reading of God's Word and proclamation based on that Word are significant emphases of Baptist worship, even though the style of worship may vary greatly.

3. Because we believe in the priesthood of all believers, the proclamation of God's Word deals with living as faithful "priests" in today's world.

4. Our understanding of the ordinances of baptism and Communion also provide a common thread for our approach to worship. The similarity in the practice of these two ordinances in Baptist churches is an affirmation of the common heritage we share. The regular gathering at the Lord's Table affirms our unity despite differences. No matter the particular understanding of Communion we bring to that table, we also affirm that Christ is the one who brings us there, and he alone truly unites us.

This session explores worship in Baptist churches. We will help children look at some of the things that make worship meaningful. We want not only to celebrate the variety of worship styles among us, but also to affirm the common foundation of praise to God that undergirds all worship.

Exploring the Biblical Basis

Psalm 95 is one of the most familiar of all the psalms. It is a joyous expression of praise for who God is and what God has done. It expresses in a minimum of words what true worship is all about.

This psalm uses a repeating pattern to call God's people into a worshiping relationship. Verses 1–2 present the invitation: "O come, let us sing to the Lord. . . ." Verses 3–5 remind listeners why this is the right thing to do: "For the Lord is a great God, and a great King above all gods. . . ." That pattern is then repeated. Verse 6 offers the invitation, "O come, let us worship and bow down . . . ," and verse 7 tells us why, "For he is our God. . . ."

Verses 1 and 2 suggest several important elements of our worshiping relationship with God. Singing, joy, thanksgiving, and praise are all parts of worship. The psalm calls us to worship, and worship is doing these things. We are important in worship, it seems to say, because of what we offer to God, not because of what is offered to us.

The reasons for worship provided in verses 3–5 and verse 7 offer another insight. Part of worship is remembering what God has done so that we can know who God is. God has created all things (the depths of the earth, the heights of the mountains, the sea, the dry land). God has cared for us and continues to care (as a shepherd cares for sheep). That is what God has done for us, that is who God is, and that is why we worship God.

Another important insight here is that God is "a great King above all gods." At first that seems like a strange affirmation for a psalm to make. After all, one of the most basic affirmations of our faith is that there is only one God. Why then do we go out of our way to say God is above all other gods? What other gods? This psalm was written in a time of competing gods, each demanding to be the object of worship. Times haven't changed. Back then they called them gods. Today the question is more subtle, but many things still compete for our allegiance, things we are tempted to make the object of our living. We place our trust in things, looking to them for security, believing they will offer us purpose and peace. We worship those things instead of God. When we are called to worship, we must remember that God is above all other gods of our own making.

As you prepare for this lesson:
Pray for each child by name. Today's class session is about encountering the holy in our lives. When we talk about worship and what makes it meaningful we are truly treading on

sacred ground. The children in your class will not be able to understand this concept fully, but they are aware of a special sense of the holy in their lives. This session will help them become more familiar with worship as celebration so that it may be more helpful to them in their own experiencing of this special sense of God's presence in their lives. As you prepare for this session offer a prayer for each of the children. Pray for help in developing and leading a session that will enable them to deepen their experience of this encounter in their own lives and together as a worshiping community.

Read and reflect on the Bible passage (Psalm 95:1–7a). You might want to use this psalm as the basis for your own devotional experience during the days before the class session. These words are very familiar. Sometimes familiarity blinds us to the full richness of meaning to be found in a passage. Read this passage over several times slowly. Focus on key words. Find a different translation to read from. As you read the psalm, think about ways the elements of worship that are mentioned happen in your own life.

Check about use of children's work in the bulletin or newsletter. During the class session, you will be writing a paraphrase of Psalm 95 to be used as an invitation to worship. Check with those responsible to see if this can be included in the church bulletin or newsletter. Knowing this will help the children in their work on the paraphrase.

Special Materials
- Party decorations

Beginning
1. *Share about parties.*
(5–10 minutes)
- Before the class begins, decorate the room for a party.
- Greet the children excitedly and with a sense of anticipation.
- When all have arrived, gather them together and say: "It looks like we're going to have a party today, doesn't it? We are, but it's going to be a different kind of party. Before I tell you what kind, though, I want to know what you like about parties."
- Ask the children to share with you the things they like about the parties they go to. As they name items, write them on newsprint or the chalkboard for all to see.

Exploring
2. *Read a story about Karly's grandmother. (10 minutes)*
- Distribute handout #10.
- Ask the children to look at the story "A Party for Karly's Grandmother."
- Introduce it by saying it is a story about a party.
- When you have finished reading the story, ask the children what Karly liked about her grandmother's party. If they name things that aren't mentioned in the list you created in Step 1, add them to the list.

3. *Talk about Psalm 95.*
(5 minutes)
- Have students turn to Psalm 95, which is printed on the handout.

- Read it aloud in an enthusiastic way. If one of the children can do this, ask him or her to read the psalm instead.
- Tell the students that this psalm is an invitation to a party.
- Ask them if they can see why.
- Explore answers the children give. If no one mentions verses 1, 2, and 6 specifically, point them out, indicating that they contain words of invitation. Say: "Just as Karly received an invitation to her grandmother's birthday celebration, these verses are an invitation to the celebration of worshiping God. But there are even more ways worship is like a party. We're going to look at some of those now."

4. *Compare a birthday celebration with a worship celebration.*
(10–15 minutes)
- Have the students turn to "When Is Worship Like a Party?" on the handout.
- On the left-hand side are a number of things that happened at Karly's grandmother's party. Review this list, making certain the children remember these things from the story.
- Have the children look again at Psalm 95. Ask them if they can see any of the same things in that psalm that are on the list. Some of these will be easy to see because the words are the same, such as *sing* and *thanksgiving*. Help the children with the ones that are more difficult: point out that the psalm talks about the good things God does and has done, just as people at the party talked about the good things Grandmother does and has done (verses 4 and 5); the psalm talks

about what God is like, just as the people at the party talked about what grandmother is like (verse 3 and 7).

■ Ask the children if they can think of things you do in your worship service that are like the party. Possible answers include: sing, bring gifts (offering), eat (communion), give thanks, tell stories (from the Bible), have speeches (the sermon).

■ Conclude by saying: "There are many ways that worship is like a celebration. Karly went to a party for her grandmother. When we go to worship, it is like going to a party for God. Just as they did for Karly's grandmother at her party, in worship we sing, we tell stories about God, we talk about why God is important to us, we offer thanks to God, and we eat. Worship is a special kind of celebration. That's the kind of party I meant for us to have today."

5. *Write an invitation to a celebration—a paraphrase of Psalm 95. (10–15 minutes)*

■ Remind the children that for Karly to go to her grandmother's party she first had to receive an invitation.

■ Have the children turn to Psalm 95 on the handout.

■ Explain that you would now like them to write an invitation to people to come to worship.

■ Tell the children that you would like to base the invitation on Psalm 95, but use different words in it. Have them use the space in the column next to the psalm to write a paraphrase. Help them by reading one verse at a time and asking the children to put its meaning into their own words. When the children have agreed on the verse's paraphrase, have them write it down and then proceed to the next verse. When you come to phrases such as "He rules over the sea, which he made . . . ," explain that the psalmist included this because it was an important thing that God did. Ask them if there are other important things God has done that they would like to include in their invitation.

■ If you have been able to arrange for this invitation to be used in the church bulletin or newsletter, tell the children when it will appear.

Responding

6. *Close by celebrating. (5 minutes)*

■ Share this thought with the children: "As Baptists, we have a long history of being concerned about worship. In the 1600s a man by the name of Obadiah Holmes journeyed from his home in Rhode Island to visit a friend who lived in Massachusetts. While he was there he helped lead a worship service in his friend's home. For that he was arrested, tried, and convicted and received twenty lashes with a whip. Fortunately, we don't have to prove it by being whipped, but worship should still be as important for us as it was for him! Being a part of the celebration of worshiping God is a great thing to be able to do!"

■ Conclude the session by reading the paraphrase of Psalm 95 that you have written.

CHAPTER 11

Issues of Faith
SPEAKING GOD'S WORD

Background for the Leader

Christians are called to share God's word with others. We do this by living out and talking about our faith. We do this as individuals, as churches, and as denominations. Because it can be difficult we don't usually think about children sharing this call with us. But this is one of the important ways they learn about and grow in their own faith. Most children will not be able to grasp all the details of policy statements, statements of concern, and other ways that different denominations attempt to speak to important issues. They can, however, appreciate the simple truth that God wants us to act and speak in loving ways and that these ways are sometimes different from the way other people act. They can also begin to understand that doing this is part of what it means to be a Christian, part of what it means to be a Baptist.

From our earliest days, Baptists have taken stands on issues of faith. Early Baptists learned that taking a stand on issues can be a difficult thing to do. Obadiah Holmes was whipped in Massachusetts for speaking God's word in a worship service held in a friend's home. Other Baptists were ridiculed and jailed for speaking in opposition to state-supported churches. Despite the difficulties, the Baptist tradition of taking a stand continues today in local churches, in regional gatherings, and in national denominational meetings.

This is not an easy thing to do. Sometimes God's word for a particular situation or issue is not clear. Sometimes people of deep faith disagree over what that word might be. Sometimes we do not say anything because we are not clear what word needs to be spoken.

Despite the difficulty and disagreements, Christians are called to speak boldly. Baptist history contains many examples of people who boldly spoke God's word. Isaac Backus spoke boldly for the separation of church and state. Prudence Crandall boldly established a school for African American women in Connecticut before the Civil War. Helen Barrett Montgomery was the first woman member of the Rochester, New York, school board, the first woman president of American Baptists, and a translator of the New Testament in a time when women did not do such things. Edwin Dahlberg boldly spoke against the evil of war. Jennie Clare Adams boldly served in a Philippine hospital and was killed with several other missionaries during World War II. Martin Luther King Jr. spoke eloquently and boldly of a dream he had for all God's people. Individual boldness is not easy. It is a great responsibility. Sometimes it is hard to discern the difference between our opinion and God's word. Sometimes

Biblical Basis
Acts 4:23–31

Objectives
By the end of the session children will be able to:
- explain how the Bible encourages us to take a stand on important issues of life and faith;
- provide a biblically based opinion about an important current issue.

Key Bible Verse
"When they had prayed . . . they were all filled with the Holy Spirit and spoke the word of God with boldness" (Acts 4:31).

we falsely assume that God has no word to speak because we can't "hear" one. Sometimes, like Jonah, we run and hide.

This session will give you and your class the opportunity to consider ways in which you can meet the challenges of speaking God's word.

Exploring the Biblical Basis

Things were not going well for the disciples. Immediately following Pentecost there had been a great burst of enthusiasm and many converts. It seemed that no power on earth would be able to stop the spread of the Good News. The believers eagerly gathered together to share their meals, to join in prayer, to worship, and to learn from the apostles. When they went out into the world, they couldn't keep silent. Transformed by their new faith, they were compelled to tell others how God's power had made a difference in their lives. That was what got them into trouble.

The trouble began when Peter and John healed a crippled beggar at the temple gate. (See session 9, "Evangelism," for a more detailed study of this story.) Peter made it worse by explaining to the crowd that the power that enabled this healing was the same power that raised the Jesus they had crucified from the dead. Such talk did not sit well with the temple authorities, so they had Peter and John arrested. With a stern warning to never again speak or teach

in the name of Jesus, Peter and John were released from prison.

The biblical basis for this session relates the events that occurred immediately following Peter and John's return to the other believers. They told their story; then with the others, they prayed that they might be able to speak God's word with boldness. The passage reports that their prayer was answered. The room in which they were gathered shook, and they were filled with the Holy Spirit and spoke the word of God.

What would you do if you had been arrested and spent the night in jail? What would you do if you were threatened by the authorities and then released on the condition that you never speak or teach again? What would you do? Like Peter, John, and the other believers, we might pray. But would our prayers be for boldness? Thanksgiving, perhaps, for our deliverance. Protection, perhaps, so that such a thing would not happen again. But boldness— to speak God's word even more boldly? This is a great prayer indeed!

It always takes boldness to speak God's word. Even though it is a word of salvation based in God's great love for us, it often does not sit well with those who hear it. Peter learned that early. And anyone who speaks God's word knows that Peter's experience is not unique. Have you known this experience?

Both the Bible and our tradition as Baptists inspire us to speak God's word boldly—

even when it is difficult, even when the response may not be a positive one. As people of faith it is our responsibility to interpret and proclaim, to witness and defend the mighty works that God is doing in our world. That's what Peter did, and all those who have followed in his footsteps. It is our heritage and our challenge.

As you prepare for this lesson:

Pray for each child by name. Ask that God will use you in the session to help children grow in their faith by learning more about how God wants them to live. If there are children you know who have particular needs, be certain to pray for them and for a strong sense of God's presence in their lives. Pray that through the experiences of this week God will enable them to come open to learning more about their faith.

Read and reflect on the Bible passage (Acts 4:23–31). For further background on the events described in this passage read Acts 3:1–4:22. It is a great story, filled with drama and excitement. Read this, as well as Acts 4:23–31, in preparation for the class, asking yourself how you would have responded in a similar situation. Also read Amos 4:1–3; 5:11–15,21–24. This will be used to provide the class with a concrete illustration of one person who was not afraid to speak out in order to show God's love for those who were in need.

Beginning

1. *Play the Should You/Would You Game. (5–10 minutes)*

■ When everyone has arrived bring the class together and tell them you want to begin by playing the "Should You/Would You Game."

■ Explain that you will describe a situation and they are to decide what they should do in that situation; then you will ask them to talk about what they really would do. As a way of encouraging their honesty with this, talk briefly about how all of us find it hard at times to do the thing we know we should do. You may want to share a personal illustration from your own life. If students see your willingness to share, they will be more willing to share themselves. Discuss the following situations one at a time:

■ A friend tells you she got a good grade on the last test because she cheated.

■ You are with a group of friends who are making fun of the boy who lives next door to you.

■ Someone comes up to your family on the street and asks for money.

You may want to describe other situations based in experiences that are familiar to students in your class.

■ When the children have finished sharing about these situations ask: "How do you decide what you *should* do in situations like this?" If no one mentions the Bible or talks about what God wants them to do, ask what role these play in their decisions.

■ Ask: "What makes it difficult to really do the things you know you should do?"

Exploring

2. *Explore shoulds and woulds for Peter. (10–15 minutes)*

■ Tell the students you are now going to look at two different people who had to make the same kind of should/would decisions. Have them turn to the "Peter's Should/Would Story" on the handout. As an introduction remind them that Peter was a fisherman who became one of Jesus' disciples, and after Jesus' resurrection he became one of the most important leaders in the church. Explain that this story tells what happened to Peter just a little while after the church was formed. Read the story together.

■ When you have finished reading, ask: "What would you do?"

■ Discuss the children's responses. Explore all the possibilities they offer, which might include: hiding, never speaking in public again, going back to the temple to heal and speak, praying, and going back to fishing.

■ Read Acts 4:23–31 together to discover what Peter really did.

■ When you have finished reading the passage, ask: "Does it surprise you that Peter prayed? Does it surprise you that Peter asked for boldness so that he could keep on speaking God's word even though the authorities had ordered him not to?"

■ Call the children's attention to the key verse: "When they had prayed . . . they were all

filled with the Holy Spirit and spoke the word of God with boldness" (Acts 4:31).

■ Note that it is through prayer that we discover what God wants us to say and gain the courage to say it.

■ Explain that this is one of many times the Bible tells us about people who spoke God's word even when it was difficult.

■ Tell the children you would like to look at another story, this one about a person in the Old Testament, who also spoke God's word.

3. *Explore shoulds and woulds for Amos. (10–15 minutes)*

■ Have the students turn to the story about Amos in the handout.

■ After reading it together, discuss with the students their ideas about what God would want Amos to say in such a situation.

■ Read the Bible passages that are listed: Amos 4:1–3; Amos 5:11–15,21–24.

■ As you read the passage in Amos 4, explore with the students the phrase "cows of Bashan" (v. 1). Ask the students what they think Amos meant by this: Was he referring to real cows or to something else?

■ Have the children read the full verse and see if they can figure it out. If no one is able to, explain that in this passage Amos is referring to the wives of the rich men in the country; they are the ones he believed oppressed the poor and crushed the needy, telling their husbands to bring them something to eat.

■ Read further to discover what Amos believed was going to

41

happen to them, noting that the word "Harmon" (v. 3) probably refers to a garbage dump.

■ Continue reading the other passages, pointing out both the way Amos condemned the ways of the people and what he said God wanted them to do.

■ Tell the children that this is very strong language, and ask: "How do you think the people would respond to Amos's words?"

■ Explain to the students that you have now looked at two different people who spoke God's word even when it was difficult.

■ Ask: "Do you think this is something everyone who believes in God should do?" Explain that churches, including Baptist churches, have tried to follow the example of Peter and Amos and speak God's word about important issues.

■ Tell the children that sometimes this can be very difficult, because people—even people who have a deep faith—don't always agree about what God wants us to say; it is also difficult because sometimes people don't like what is said.

Responding

4. *Decide what issues the church should speak about.* (5–10 minutes)

■ Tell the students that they are going to do something that will help them decide about speaking God's word on an important issue.

■ Ask them to turn to the section titled "Should the church speak about . . ." on the handout.

■ Point out the list of issues. You may want to add some of your own.

■ Explain to the children that their first job is to decide which of these issues the church should say something about.

■ Remind them that another way of looking at this question is to ask: "Does God have a special word for us to say about this issue?"

■ Note that answering this question was what led both Peter and Amos to decide to speak.

■ Go over the list, asking students to share their opinions and the reasons for them. They do not all have to agree about each issue. What is important here is that they do their own thinking about issues that are important to our faith.

5. *Decide what you would say.* (5 minutes)

■ Once you have completed discussing the list, ask each student to pick one of the issues he or she thinks the church should speak about.

■ Give the children several minutes to write down what they think the church should say about the issue they selected.

■ If time allows, have students share their thoughts with one another. They may not all agree on the opinions that are shared. If this is the case, point out that this is one of the reasons it is difficult for churches to speak God's word on issues in today's world, but we must try to follow the examples of Peter and Amos and speak out.

■ Explain that this is one of the important characteristics of Baptists.

■ Say: "Our church, along with other Baptist churches all around the country, has a long tradition of seeking to speak God's word on important issues. We do this as individual churches and as a group of churches. It's not always easy to do this, but part of what it means to be a Baptist is to work together to discover what God wants us to say about important issues of faith, just like Peter and Amos did. This isn't just for churches, either. Each one of us also needs to think about what God wants us to say and share that word with others."

6. *Close with prayer.* (5 minutes)

■ Close with a prayer thanking God for the example of people like Peter and Amos, who show us what it means to speak God's word.

■ Ask God for courage to speak with the same kind of boldness that they did.

CHAPTER 12

Prophetic Role
BEING GOD'S PEOPLE

Background for the Leader

Christians face a great challenge today—living in a non-Christian world. How do we speak and act as disciples in a culture that is in many ways alien to the gospel? This is a prophetic challenge that involves speaking and living out God's Word so that the world sees, hears, and understands the gospel. Baptists have a long tradition of speaking a prophetic word even when it goes against societal norms. We began by challenging government interference in personal faith, and we continue to apply the gospel to societal issues. In this session we will look at ways Baptists, both as individuals and with others, have played this prophetic role of bringing God's Word to the world.

Baptists were born a prophetic people. From the very beginning they brought God's Word to bear on the significant issues of life. Baptists began as a people of protest; they stood against the usual and customary ways of thinking and acting. When others believed a civil society was impossible without a state religion, Baptists founded a colony that granted full liberty of conscience in matters of religion.

Roger Williams in Providence and John Clarke in Newport were prophets of a new way to understand relationships between the state and the church. This prophetic call was taken up in later times by John Leland in Virginia and Isaac Backus in Massachusetts. It continues to be a Baptist witness today.

While religious freedom was our first, and perhaps greatest, prophetic witness, it is not our only one. Baptists stood tall against the evil of slavery, even though it meant the division of our historic mission societies. Baptists have been prophets of peace in the midst of violence, prophets of justice in the midst of oppression, and prophets of hope in the midst of despair and destruction. Charles Evans Hughes, as secretary of state, and Edwin Dahlberg, as a pastor, were both prophets of peace in the world. Isabel Crawford, as a missionary to the Kiowas, and Walter Rauschenbusch, as a seminary professor and author, were both prophets of social justice. Baptists today continue to proclaim a prophetic message about what it means at the beginning of the twenty-first century to live as people who share the Christian faith.

The prophet's role is not an easy one. It is difficult for the individual, perhaps even more so for a denomination. First, it is a matter of seeking God's word, of discovering what God is saying in a particular time and place about a particular situation or issue. Even if one person has a strong sense of this word, there is still the need to have it tested within the community of faith. For a denomination the process

Biblical Basis
1 Peter 2:1–12

Objectives
By the end of the session children will be able to:
- describe what it means to be a chosen race, God's own people;
- state ways in which they are and will live as God's chosen people.

Key Bible Verse
"You are a chosen race, a royal priesthood, a holy nation, God's own people, in order that you may proclaim the mighty acts of him who called you out of darkness into his marvelous light" (1 Peter 2:9).

of developing a sense of God's word in the midst of often opposing views is arduous and seemingly impossible. If the word becomes clear, if it is sustained in testing, there still remains the challenge of speaking it clearly and of living it. All of this can drain the spirit of even the most faithful among us.

Despite the difficulties, Baptists continued to assume the prophetic role that comes with being God's people. This is our heritage, a heritage that both challenges and inspires us as we live in a world that continues so often to be at odds with the Good News.

Exploring the Biblical Basis

Early Christians knew what it was like to live in a world that was alien to the gospel, a world in which only a minority professed, shared, and lived by the Christian faith. Living a Christian life put them at odds with all other major religions of the day. Even Judaism, the faith from which they grew, offered hostile opposition to their existence. Yet Christians continued to proclaim God's Word, to share God's love, and to grow as churches. It wasn't easy. The First Letter of Peter was written to these early Christians in the midst of their struggle and persecution. It offers both encouragement and challenge. In the words of *The New Interpreter's Bible*, ". . . the epistle helps to strengthen Christians in times of distress; sets their lives within the history of God's activity, which moves from

creation to consummation; holds up the atoning death of Jesus Christ; and encourages mutual love among Christian people and forbearance of enemies."[1] Peter describes the reality early Christians faced and calls the early followers of Christ to faithfulness.

The passage that is our focus in this session spans two sections of Peter's letter. Verses 1–10 conclude a section that describes God's holy people. Verses 11–12 begin a section on what it means for Christians to live in an alien world of nonbelievers. Thus, we see in it both an affirming description of the faithful and an inspiring challenge to faithful living. This challenge is a call to speak and live a prophetic word.

The passage begins by listing the negative qualities Christians should set aside and describing what they should seek in their lives. Malice, guile, insincerity, envy, and slander are destructive to the community and make growing in faith impossible. They can be countered, much as a mother's milk protects a baby from infection, by "pure, spiritual milk" that enables growth in salvation.

Verses 4 through 8 use the image of "living stones" being "built into a spiritual house" to affirm a close relationship between God's work in Christ and in them. Peter reminds his readers of the ease with which the world rejects the faith, and he encourages them to remain faithful despite rejection. Believers can do this by offering "spiritual sacrifices acceptable to God" and remaining obedient to God's Word.

Verse 9, which is the key verse for this session, boldly affirms who Christians are and what they are to do. Christians are "a chosen race, a royal priesthood, a holy nation, God's own people" so that they might "proclaim the mighty acts" of God. This purpose goes beyond their own salvation; they are called to play a prophetic role for God.

God's mighty acts are not simply what God has done in Jesus Christ, as wondrous as that is. They also include God's continuing work in the world—calling them and us "out of darkness into his marvelous light." That work carries on as others are called to the light as God's love is shared, as God's kingdom comes. This is a biblical warrant for our lives as a prophetic people.

Attempts to respond to God's prophetic call often become divisive within churches and denominations. This passage makes an important affirmation that helps us deal with this reality. It is a theme that runs throughout these verses but is most clearly stated at the beginning: "Rid yourselves, therefore, of all malice, and all guile, insincerity, envy, and all slander." These are words about the way in which members of the Christian community are to treat each other. This theme is picked up again in verses 11 and 12. The "desires of the flesh" are not limited to those of a sensual nature. They include all sins that spring from a focus on self, turning one away from others and from God. This self-centered behavior is precisely that which the author encourages us to set aside in verse 1. The reason for this is clearly stated in verse 12: More than a matter of personal purity, it is so nonbelievers "may see your honorable deeds and glorify God when he comes to judge." The way we treat one another is one of our greatest witnesses to the power of God's love. It is one of the clearest prophetic words we can speak in a world in which love is so often lacking in relationships, especially among those who disagree with one another.

As you prepare for this lesson:

Pray for each child by name. During the week focus your thoughts and prayers on each child. You may want to focus on several children each day of the week. Think about them, their family situations, and the lives they have before them. Consider what it might mean for each of them to grow in an awareness of what it means to be a prophet for God. Pray that this class session may be an important part of that kind of growth in their lives.

Read and reflect on the Bible passage (1 Peter 2:1–12). Although 1 Peter is less well known than some of the other New Testament epistles, many will be familiar with the passage that is the basis for this session. Its dramatic imagery makes it perhaps the best-known passage in 1 Peter. The letter itself is not long. You may want to read it in its entirety. If that is not possible, take time to read 2:1–12 and the "Exploring the Biblical

Basis" section of this guide. This will provide essential information for your teaching.

Special Materials
- A doughnut or other snack
- A mop or broom

Beginning

1. *Consider what it means to be chosen. (5 minutes)*
- Welcome the children to class.
- Tell them you need two people to do some special things for you this morning.
- If some children volunteer and others don't, select one from those who do and the other from those who don't. (Based on your knowledge of the children in the class, select ones you think are more likely to follow your directions and be able to reflect on the experience with the class.) Give one person a doughnut or other snack and ask him or her to eat it. Hand the other person the mop or broom and ask him or her to sweep the floor in your classroom.
- When the children have finished their assignments, use these questions to guide a discussion.
- Ask the two you chose: "How did it feel to be chosen?" "How did it feel when you found out what I wanted you to do?" Ask the rest of the children in the class: "How did you feel when I didn't choose you?" "When you found out that one of the assignments was sweeping the floor, how did you feel?"
- Conclude this step with words such as these: "Being chosen is a

strange thing. Most of us like to be chosen when we're playing a game or doing something fun, but we don't like to be chosen to do something that is unpleasant. Today we're going to look at a Bible passage that tells us God has chosen us. That's good. But when we learn what it is that God has chosen us to do, we may discover that it's not always easy or fun."

Exploring

2. *Explore the Bible passage. (5–10 minutes)*
- Distribute handout #12.
- Read the key verse.
- Point out that this verse uses four different phrases to talk about how God has chosen us. Ask the students to say what they are (a chosen race, a royal priesthood, a holy nation, God's own people).
- Ask: "What does this passage say is the reason for our being chosen?" (". . . to proclaim the mighty acts of him who called you out of darkness into his marvelous light.") If the children need help in understanding the meaning of this image you might explain it in some of these ways: the darkness represents our sin, and the light is the forgiveness we have in Christ; darkness is life without Christ, and the light is new life with Christ; darkness is feeling separated from God, and light is feeling close to God.
- Ask: "How do you feel about being chosen for that?"
- Explain that this verse is part of a passage that deals with the way Christians are supposed to live.

■ Ask the students to turn to 1 Peter 2:1–12 in their Bibles. Tell them that much of this passage is made up of quotations from other parts of the Bible, but that our main interest is the text that isn't quotes.

■ Tell the students that the passage begins by saying what Christians aren't supposed to do. Ask them to name some of these things. These are found in verse 1.

■ Read verses 11 and 12. Ask: "Why do you think Christians are 'aliens and strangers'?" (because the way God wants us to live is different from the way most people live).

■ Explain that the phrase "desires of the flesh" refers to the selfishness that keeps us concerned about ourselves, rather than about other people and God.

■ Use words such as these to conclude this step: "So far, we've seen what God's chosen people *aren't* supposed to be. There are a lot of passages in the Bible that talk about what they *are* supposed to be. Let's look at some of them now."

3. *Describe God's chosen people. (5 minutes)*
■ Have students turn to "How Do God's People Live?" on the handout.
■ Go over the directions.
■ Read the Bible passages and use them to complete the word game. The solution is shown at right.
■ Conclude this step with words such as these: "Now we've got an idea about the way it's supposed to be if you're one of

God's chosen people. Let's see what it's like when people really live that way."

4. *Develop and present scenes from "The Chosen Ones." (25–30 minutes)*
■ Tell the students you are going to produce a play called "The Chosen Ones."
■ Divide the class into two groups. On the handout they will find the script for several scenes from the lives of Walter Rauschenbusch and Ann Hasseltine Judson.
■ Explain that these are two Baptists who found out what it meant to live as God's chosen people in their own lives and times.

■ Assign one name to each group.
■ Give the groups about 5 minutes to develop scenes to go along with the script. These can involve movement, or they can be still, as if they were slides with the script as the caption.
■ When the groups have completed their preparation, have them present their productions to each other.
■ When the presentations are over, affirm both groups.
■ Talk with the children about the ways in which these two people acted like God's chosen people. Say something such as this: "We've looked at two people's lives, but they lived a long time ago. There's still a need for

Answers to How Do God's People Live?

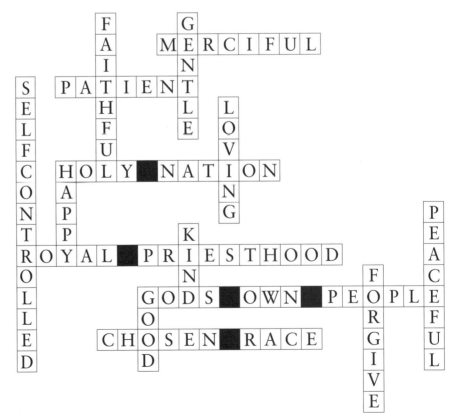

46

people like this today. Let's think about some ways people today can be God's chosen people."

■ Read "Debra at School" and "Josh at Home."

■ Divide the class into two groups again and assign one story to each group. Ask them to develop a brief skit that shows what Debra and Josh might do in the situations that are described.

■ Allow 5 minutes for them to prepare and then have each group share. Discuss each presentation when it is over. "Josh at Home" raises the possibility of physical abuse in the home. Be sensitive to the way the students respond to this. If the discussion raises concerns that need to be dealt with further, talk with your pastor.

Responding

5. *Share ways to be God's people. (5 minutes)*

■ Remind the group of the various things you have done in this session.

■ Tell them that what matters most is not what anyone else does, but what they do.

■ Work together to develop a brainstorming list of things they can do to act like God's chosen people. These may be things that were mentioned in the Bible passage or illustrated in the skits or things that they think of on their own.

6. *Close with prayer. (5 minutes)*

■ Review the list you have developed and encourage the students to do these things even more than they are now.

■ Close with a prayer that names some of these qualities specifically and asks for God's help in doing them in order to act more fully as God's chosen people.

Note

1. David L. Bartlett, "1 Peter," *The New Interpreter's Bible* (Nashville: Abingdon, 1998), 12:233.

CHAPTER 13

Diversity
TOGETHER, EVEN THOUGH WE'RE DIFFERENT

Background for the Leader

Diversity is and always has been a reality. People are different—in dress, values, skin color, and language. Even Christians have differences. We have a variety of ideas about what meaningful worship is and about the church and its purpose. Every day we are confronted by the differences that abound in the world and are thus challenged to search for common bonds that bring us together. When we find common bonds, it becomes easier for us to affirm our differences rather than fear them. This is true in society. It is also true in the church. Just as there is diversity within churches of different denominations, there is diversity among Baptist churches as well. The purpose of this session is to discover some of the differences that exist and to affirm the common bonds that hold us together. In this way our differences can be seen more clearly as a source of strength and a reason for celebration.

In the United States racial/ethnic diversity is increasing along with the awareness that diversity exists. The Asian and Hispanic populations of the United States have seen significant growth in recent years, and African Americans and Native Americans play a more significant role in the discussion of what and who our nation is than they did even in the recent past. These factors have a significant impact on all of us. They make us aware of change and of the fact that change is often difficult to manage. They cause us to wonder what common bonds unite us when the common values, color, and heritage that once held communities together no longer work. They create fear because differences make it more difficult to understand, to communicate, to care.

The other side to this coin of diversity is that as it grows we become more aware of it, and we open ourselves to the possibility of being enriched by the experience and gifts of others. Whether it be something as simple as food or as complex as an understanding of relationships, diversity offers to us the opportunity to learn from each other and grow together.

What is true culturally is also true denominationally. Most Baptist denominations are becoming more diverse. Once predominantly white, American Baptist Churches in the U.S.A. may soon be a denomination in which no racial/ethnic group has majority status. Statistics can't tell the whole story, but they do help us begin to see the picture of a new and growing reality. In 1995 resident membership of American Baptist churches was 53 percent Euro-American, 42 percent African American, 3 percent Hispanic, 1 percent Asian, and .1 percent Native American.

Biblical Basis
Acts 10:34–35 and Galatians 3:26–29

Objectives
By the end of the session children will be able to:
- describe a way diversity was handled in the early church;
- state the contribution several people of different racial and ethnic backgrounds have made to the life and mission of Baptists.

Key Bible Verse
"So there is no difference between Jews and Gentiles, between slaves and free men, between men and women; you are all one in union with Christ Jesus" (Galatians 3:28, TEV).

Recent years demonstrate a clear trend of a decline in Euro-American members and an increase in all others.[1] This diversity is both a reason for great celebration and a great challenge.

We celebrate the fact that Baptist roots are deeply set in different racial/ethnic communities. All in their own way have found something in being Baptist that enables an important expression of who they are and who they believe God is. We celebrate the fact that Baptists, for a number of reasons but largely because of our historic emphasis on local church autonomy, have long been a diverse group of people. Significant differences have always existed among us, but we still have found ways to be together. We celebrate the richness of our diverse heritage that enables us to enrich our own faith through interaction with and learning from others. We celebrate the great opportunity we have as Baptists to work out our relationships in a context of diversity and recognize that as we do so within the church, we enable it to happen within society.

One challenge we face is to change old patterns in order to enable new relationships. Another is to continue to affirm the common bonds that unite us even amid great differences. As Christians we must grow together as a whole people of God and not become isolated pockets of homogeneity. We can begin to meet these challenges by becoming more aware and more affirming of the diversity that exists in our own congregations,

whether racial/ethnic diversity or diversity of another kind, such as in worship or music styles, theology, age groupings, or something as basic as a difference of opinion about the proper dress for worship. Any diversity calls us as God's people and as Baptists to seek the common bonds that unite us despite our differences and asks us to find an openness to one another that enables us to affirm and learn from our differences.

Exploring the Biblical Basis

In this session we turn to Peter and Paul to discover how they handled the issue of diversity within the early church.

The background for Peter's affirmation of Acts 10:34–35 is found in the story that begins with Acts 10:1. Cornelius was a Roman centurion stationed in Caesarea, the Roman headquarters in Palestine. He had shown interest in the Jewish religion and probably had adopted many of their practices, although he had not converted to Judaism. One afternoon he had a vision in which he clearly saw an angel of God and heard the angel direct him to make contact with Peter. He immediately sent his servants in search of Peter. The next day Peter had a vision; this one was a bit more difficult to interpret. While resting on the roof of the house where he was staying, Peter saw what appeared to be a large sheet descending from heaven. In it were a variety of animals that Jews, according to their dietary laws, were not

allowed to eat. A voice commanded, "Get up, Peter; kill and eat." Peter protested, knowing that it was against the Jewish law, but the voice continued until the sheet was taken back up into heaven. While Peter pondered the meaning of this vision, word came of the arrival of Cornelius's servants. After hearing their story, Peter went with them to Caesarea, where Cornelius warmly greeted him and described his vision. Peter's reply begins in Acts 10:34–35: "I now realize that it is true that God treats all men alike. Whoever fears him and does what is right is acceptable to him, no matter what race he belongs to" (TEV). The vision was a call to Peter to move beyond the common bond of the law to a new common bond, faith in Christ; to embrace a new diversity of race among God's people.

Paul also dealt with the issue of diversity within the early church. He was the strongest advocate of the mission to the Gentiles. Paul did all he could to incorporate them into the body of Christ without imposing the Jewish law upon them. For Paul, too, there was to be a new common bond, faith in Christ. In the Letter to the Galatians, Paul was writing to a church that upset him by listening to a group that claimed followers of Christ must also observe the Jewish law. Throughout the letter he is strong in his condemnation of this view. Repeatedly, Paul sounds the theme of unity in Christ despite social or cultural differences. His strongest affirmation of this view is our passage: "So there is no difference between Jews and Gentiles, between slaves and free men, between men and women; you are all one in union with Christ Jesus" (Galatians 3:28, TEV). In Christ the old distinctions do not disappear; they just don't count for anything anymore. One is still Jew or Greek, slave or free, man or woman, but it doesn't make any difference in the eyes of God or in the eyes of believers. Being together in Christ is such a strong bond of unity that all differences become irrelevant. This becomes the standard by which Christians treat each other.

As you prepare for this lesson:

Pray for each child by name.
This session is about people who are different from us. Differences often prompt interest, but they can also provoke fear. We do not understand that which is different; what we do not understand we often fear. In that fear lies a tendency to view those who are different as wrong or perhaps as a threat. Even children understand this reality of human nature. They realize differences that exist among people, and they have experienced some of the fear that is associated with those differences. They have seen what happens to other children because they have a different color of skin or are of a different race, weight, or level of intelligence. And yet, God created the world full of differences, so that we might enjoy them and our lives be enriched

by them. Knowing this encourages us to be open to different people, different ways, and different ideas, even if we may not understand them. Be aware of this tension between fear and openness in yourself and your students as you prepare for this session. Offer a prayer for each of the children as they deal with diversity. Pray for help in developing and leading a session that will enable them to deepen their appreciation of diversity in their lives, in the church, and among Baptists.

Read and reflect on the Bible passages (Acts 10:34–35; Galatians 3:26–29). Read both passages that are the Bible basis for this session. It will also be especially helpful to read Acts 10:1–11:18. This will give you the full story of Peter and Cornelius and the important role their relationship played in enabling diversity within the early church. If you have time, read the entire Letter to the Galatians. It is only six chapters and provides a wonderful affirmation of the common bond Christians share in Christ, along with stern warnings about falling away from Christ as the basis for our unity.

Select a song. Select an appropriate song to use in the closing; a suggestion is made in Step 5.

Beginning

1. *Explore differences.*
(10 minutes)
■ Welcome the children as they arrive in class.
■ Begin by explaining that today you will be looking at ways

people are different, especially in the church.
■ Distribute handout #13, asking the children to look at "I'm Different!"
■ Review the directions. They have three minutes to move around the room finding people who are different from them in each of the areas that are listed. Make sure everyone has something to write with and tell them to begin.
■ After three minutes call time. Have the children share some of the things they discovered.
■ Explain that this game helped them find out ways members of the class are different from one another.
■ Ask the children to think about their school and see if they can name additional ways children are different from one another there. List these on newsprint or the chalkboard.
■ Ask the class to think about the whole world and even more ways people are different. List their responses on newsprint or the chalkboard. Possibilities include different countries, languages, races, food, governments, kinds of houses.
■ Tell the children you want them to think about another place in which people are different from one another: the church. Ask them to name as many ways people are different from one another in your church as they can. List their responses on newsprint or the chalkboard. Possibilities include different ages, different Sunday school classes, different tastes in music, different jobs held in the church.

■ Have the children look at all the lists of differences. Ask: "With all these differences, how do we ever get along together?"

■ Explore answers that the children offer. If someone suggests that we also have things in common with one another, explore what those might be.

■ Call their attention to the church, asking: "What about in the church? What brings us together here? What do we have in common?"

Exploring

2. *Read a story about Peter and Cornelius. (10–15 minutes)*

■ Tell the children that one of the most important issues for the church right after Jesus' resurrection was that people in the church were so different from one another.

■ Ask them to look at the story about Peter and Cornelius on the handout as you read it.

■ Read the first two paragraphs of the story, and then ask and discuss these questions:
— What is a vision? (It's like a dream, except you're not sleeping.)
— What do you think the meaning of Peter's vision was?

■ After ideas are shared, say: "Let's keep reading, and we'll find out what the answer is."

■ Read the next paragraph, and then ask and discuss these questions:
— Who do you think was responsible for these visions? (The writer of Acts believes that God was.)
— What would you think if someone showed up at your

house saying that he had a vision in which God told him to come see you? (Let the children share their thoughts, explaining that there are no right or wrong answers for this one.)

■ Read the fourth paragraph, and then ask and discuss these questions:
— What was unusual about Cornelius's becoming a Christian? (He was one of the first people to become a Christian who wasn't Jewish and didn't follow all the Jewish laws, including those about which foods could be eaten.)
— When Peter heard about Cornelius's vision and that he wanted to become a Christian, he understood the meaning of his own vision. What was it? (Christians don't all have to eat the same food. What Christians have in common is belief in Christ and a desire to grow in relationship with Christ.)

3. *Explore our diverse Baptist heritage. (15–20 minutes)*

■ Introduce this step with a statement such as this: "Peter helped the early church understand that all kinds of people could be Christians. Because he did, people of all races and cultures, rich people and poor people, famous people and ordinary people all became members of the church. The only thing they needed to have in common was a desire to know Jesus. That's been true ever since Peter's time. Our church is a Baptist church. There are many differences among Baptists. We're going

to do something now that will help us discover something about the different kinds of people who have been Baptists in the past. They did different things. They were from different races. They were men and women. But what they had in common was faith in Jesus, just like Cornelius and Peter."

■ Tell the children that you are going to give them a few minutes to do some research about famous Baptists; when you come back together you will pretend to be one of the people they researched, and they will have the chance to ask you questions to discover who you are.

■ Have the class look at "Famous Baptists" on the handout.

■ Divide the class into several groups, up to a total of six.

■ Assign each of the groups one person to research. Since there are eight people, there will be at least two people that do not have groups assigned to them.

■ Allow two or three minutes for the research.

■ After the allotted time, bring the class back together. Tell them you are a famous Baptist. Allow each group to ask you one question about who you are. It must be a question you can answer yes or no. If you answer yes, the group may ask another question. If you answer no, the next group gets to ask a question.

■ Answer the questions based on the material provided in the handout.

■ When one of the students figures out who you are, have him or her read the paragraph about you to the other children.

- Then select another person to "be," and play the guessing game again. To make this game more challenging, choose one of the people who was not researched or pretend to be someone in your church.

4. *Discover what keeps us together. (5–10 minutes)*
- Congratulate the children for their good work in guessing the various people you were.
- Remind them that the purpose of this game was to help them learn more about the different people who are and have been Baptists.
- Put this into your own words as a way of sharing the key Bible verse with the class: "We've already looked at Peter and discovered that he wanted to included different kinds of people in the church. Another person who lived at the same time and worked at this was Paul. In one of his letters to a church he reminded the members that the only thing they really needed to have in common was their faith in Christ. He said that if they had this, all the ways that they were different wouldn't matter any more.
- Have the class turn to Galatians 3:26–29 in their Bibles. Read it together as an affirmation of being together in Christ, even though we are different in so many ways.

Responding
5. *Close with prayer and a song. (5 minutes)*
- Close this session with a prayer thanking God for all the differences in the world and for the common bond we share in Christ, which brings us together even though we are not all alike.
- Sing a song that celebrates our differences, such as "Jesus Loves the Little Children."

Note
1. Percentages prepared by David Cushman based on the 1995 Annual Reports of the ABC/USA by using simple linear regression with about twenty years of figures from the Congregational Profile System database.

CHAPTER 14

Mission
SHARING GOOD NEWS
HERE, THERE, AND EVERYWHERE

Background for the Leader

Baptists are a mission people: they desire to engage in mission. The realization that the challenge of mission was too great for any single church led to the beginnings of Baptist denominational life. Churches united, and together they formed the foreign and home mission societies. They worked to publish resources to distribute and to reach people for Christ. This zeal for mission continues. Mission is more than just what national and regional organizations do, however. Because many people do not attend church, America is one of the world's greatest mission fields. Increasingly, the local congregation is seen as a mission outpost.

At one time mission was something that happened "out there"—in the place to which we sent missionaries. We gave our financial support so missionaries could be sent. We listened to the verbal and written reports of the great work made possible because of our giving. But most of the time we had little direct involvement in mission ourselves. "Out there" might be

in Africa or Asia, or any foreign land, among people who had not had the opportunity we had to learn about Christ. Or, it might be here in our own country among people who were seen as "needy." Most often, however, we didn't think about mission as happening in our own communities, in our own churches, through our Sunday school and our worship service.

All that has changed. Mission still happens "out there," but now it is clear that it happens, it must happen, "right here," too. We live in an unchurched society. Well over half of our fellow citizens have no significant relationship to a church. Our friends and neighbors, just as much as those halfway around the world, are in need of Christian missionary presence in their lives so they can come to know the saving grace of Jesus Christ.

This means that our understanding of mission—where it happens, how it happens, and who does it—is expanding. Baptist national and regional mission agencies are still vitally important in our worldwide mission effort. They do things no single church could ever

accomplish on its own. But now the mission work of the local congregation has taken on new meaning. Virtually every church is a mission outpost in its community, seeking to be a Christian presence in a culture and society that does not know, but needs to know, the Good News.

This expanded understanding of mission has many implications. Denominational structures were created to support mission "out there." Now, structure is

Biblical Basis
Acts 1:6–11

Objectives
By the end of the session children will be able to:
- describe different ways the Good News can be shared with others;
- talk about at least one way they witness for Jesus by sharing the Good News.

Key Bible Verse
"You will be my witnesses in Jerusalem, in all Judea and Samaria, and to the ends of the earth" (Acts 1:8).

needed, both within the denomination and the congregation, to ensure that mission happens "right here" as well. Mission giving used to be something separate from the local budget of the church. Now that distinction is no longer as clear. Money used to support the congregation is as much mission giving as is money sent to support a missionary in another country. Both are important. Both are essential. But this is a different way to think about it.

Mission has always been a driving force in Baptist life. Adoniram Judson, the first Baptist missionary from America, was half way to India before Bible study led him to a belief in believer's baptism. Once Baptists in the United States learned they already had a Baptist missionary on the field, they embraced Judson and his passion for mission. Soon the American Baptist Foreign Mission Society was formed in 1814 to support his work. Similar passion led to the development of the Home Mission Society in 1832. Reaching people for Christ also happens through the printed word and through education. So a passion for mission led to the founding of the American Baptist Publication Society, another mission organization. Over the years, as regional groupings of churches in associations and state conventions developed, a passion for mission led them into important work within their own areas. This same passion for mission is at work in new ways today, with a special focus on the local congregation. Baptists are a missionary people. We

always have been, and by God's grace, we always will be.

Children will not need to know, and will not be able to comprehend, all the changes that are taking place in our understanding of mission. What they can grasp, however, is a very important lesson. They can understand that mission is what witnesses do to share Jesus with others. And they can understand that they are able to do that, just the same as people who serve as missionaries in countries all around the world.

Exploring the Biblical Basis

The disciples were playing a waiting game. Ever since the amazing day on which Jesus rose from the dead, they had waited—waited for Jesus to appear to them again, waited for the promised coming of God's Spirit. Jesus did come. One last time. They knew it was a special time, and so they asked the question that had been on their minds for days now. "Is this the time you will restore the king dom to Israel?" In other words, "Is this the time you will make it the way it used to be for us?" Jesus answered by telling them not to worry about time schedules—this was God's concern, not theirs. But then he went on, telling them what they should be doing until God's time was fulfilled. "You will be my witnesses," he said, "in Jerusalem, in all Judea and Samaria, and to the ends of the earth." To paraphrase, "You will be the ones who tell the world about

God's work and love, about the great things God has done and continues to do, about the promise God made that can now be claimed by everyone. You will witness to all of that in what you say and in what you do everywhere you go."

Then, ascending into heaven, Jesus left them. And there they stood gazing after him until two messengers from God came along and said, "What are you doing standing here? There's work to be done!"

In this day when the whole notion of what mission is and how and where it happens is being reconsidered, these words of Jesus are especially important for us. Like the disciples, we too, may be longing for past greatness—the way things used to be. Jesus ignores our concern, not out of callousness, but because he knows there is something more important for us to be about. Instead, he directs our attention to the task at hand— being his witnesses. We start where we are. For the disciples it was Jerusalem; for us it may well be our own community. From there we go where Jesus points the way: to Judea, the surrounding country-side; to Samaria, the neighboring, yet alien and somewhat hostile territory; and on to the ends of the earth. Like the disciples, we may hear these words and be overwhelmed, so much so that we just stand there. We plan but don't move. We talk but don't act. We gaze into the skies wondering what possible difference we can make. But for us, too, there must come the time when we hear the words, perhaps spoken by another, perhaps spoken within our own hearts, "What are you doing standing here? There's work to be done!"

As you prepare for this lesson:

Pray for each child by name.
This session is about putting our faith into action by becoming involved in mission. Children are involved in mission in a number of ways, both by supporting the mission work of others and by doing mission themselves. They have regular opportunities to give to special mission offerings. They can also be involved in mission as they play with friends and interact within their families. They don't think about it this way, of course, but it is mission if they are sharing God's love with others. As you think about the children in your class during the week, pray for this mission involvement that they already have. Pray also that this class session might lead them into fuller participation in God's mission in the world.

Read and reflect on the Bible passage (Acts 1:6–11). Read the Bible passage we will be studying. Reflect on the places that are comparable to Jerusalem, Judea, and Samaria in your life and the lives of your students. Think about the ways people are and can be witnesses for Christ.

Special Materials

■ map or globe to point out Alaska and South India (optional)

■ drawing paper for Step 5 (optional)

Beginning

1. *Share good news. (5 minutes)*
■ Welcome the children and tell them you would like to begin by sharing good news about things that happened this past week. Start by sharing either about something good that happened in your personal life or something good that happened in your community or the world that the children might have heard about.
■ Ask the children to share some good news, too.
■ When the sharing is finished, say something such as: "I like hearing good news. It makes me feel happy. It gives me hope. Thank you for sharing your good news with me."

Exploring

2. *Read Jimmy's story. (10–15 minutes)*
■ Tell the children you want to read a story about a boy who had a lot of bad news in his life but was finally able to have some good news to share.
■ Distribute handout #14 and ask the children to look at "Jimmy's Story."
■ Read or have someone in the class read the first two paragraphs. If you have a map or globe, point out where you live and then show the children where Alaska is.
■ Ask: "What feelings do you think Jimmy had that made him want to run away? Have you ever felt that way? Why do you

think Jimmy decided running away wasn't going to solve his problems?"
■ Read the next two paragraphs.
■ Tell the children that the Jesse Lee Home and Alaska Children's Service are among the ways that Baptists share good news with other people. By working together, churches support the home so that children like Jimmy will have a place to live.
■ Read the next paragraph.
■ Ask: "What do you think was the most important thing that happened to Jimmy at the Jesse Lee Home?"
■ Read the rest of the story.
■ Ask: "Do you think it took a lot of courage for Jimmy to stand up in church and say what he did? Why do you think he did it? What was the good news for Jimmy in this story?"

3. *Read the Bible passage and play "Witness Scramble." (10–15 minutes)*
■ Tell the children that you want to read a Bible passage that helps explain why churches do things such as support the Jesse Lee Home so that people like Jimmy will have a chance to change their lives.
■ Ask the class to turn to Acts 1:6–11 in their Bibles. Provide background information about the passage by saying something such as this: "Acts was written by the same person who wrote Luke. Luke is the story of Jesus' life and death and resurrection. Acts picks up the story after Easter, telling about what Jesus' followers did then. The passage we're going to read is the story

of the last time Jesus was with his followers before he went back to heaven. The things he said then are very important."

■ Have someone read the passage, or read it yourself. Highlight some of the important points by saying something such as: "Jesus' last instructions to his followers were that they were to be witnesses in Jerusalem (the city they were in) and all around the world. A witness is somebody who tells people about something they have seen or know. A witness for Jesus Christ is a person who tells others about who Jesus is and what Jesus has done. Sometimes a witness uses words to talk about Jesus. Sometimes a witness shows others what Jesus has done by acting in the same loving, caring way Jesus acted."

■ Tell the class that there are many ways to be witnesses for Jesus.

■ Have the children turn to "Witness Unscramble" on the handout.

■ Explain the directions and have them begin. Divide the class into teams of two or three to work on this, or have them do it individually. The correct answers are: care, serve, share the good news, love, help others, mission, tell about Jesus, invite friends to church.

■ When they have unscrambled the letters, encourage the children to come up with other things a witness for Jesus does, scramble the words, and challenge the others to unscramble them.

■ When they have finished, ask the children to think about "Jimmy's Story."

■ Ask: "Did the people who helped Jimmy do any of these things? Were they witnesses for Jesus?"

4. *Read Sandy's story.*
(5 minutes)

■ Tell the class you would like to read another story about a person who is a witness.

■ Read or have some in the class read "Sandy's Story."

■ Ask the class to name as many things as they can that Sandy does.

■ Ask: "Are these the things a witness does? Is Sandy a witness for Jesus? Why?"

Responding

5. *Decide ways to share Good News. (10–15 minutes)*

■ Tell the class that witnesses do many different things. What makes them witnesses for Jesus is that by what they say or by what they do they share the Good News of Jesus' love for everyone.

■ Ask the children whether they think they are witnesses for Jesus.

■ Explore with the class some things they can do to share the Good News about Jesus' love with others.

■ Have them use the space that is provided on the handout to draw a picture of at least one thing they do to be a witness for Jesus by sharing good news, or distribute drawing paper and ask the children to be witnesses by making "good news cards" to send to the children at homes such as the one where Jimmy stayed.

6. *Close with prayer.*
(5 minutes)

■ Bring the class back together.

■ Ask those who wish to share their art work and tell what they do to be witnesses.

■ Explain that people all around the world are witnesses for Jesus.

■ Remind the children that you have talked about how they are witnesses right here, how the people who helped Jimmy were witnesses in Alaska, and how Sandy was a witness in South India.

■ Close with a prayer thanking God for everyone who is a witness and asking for God's help in being witnesses every day.

Handouts

Soul Freedom
I DECIDE ABOUT JESUS

Bible Basis Matthew 16:13–16
Key Bible Verse "Who do you say that I am?"
(Matthew 16:15).

The Boy and the Professors

Everyone was impressed. In fact, they couldn't
believe it. The college students all gathered
around the young boy who sat in the dining
room talking to three professors. He looked
like he was twelve years old, but he knew
more than the professors! He talked about
law and government. He talked about religion. He even talked about math and science.
The professors couldn't believe it either. Some
of them even got angry that this little kid
knew more than they did. They tried to trick
him and prove that he was wrong about
things, but they couldn't.

What would people say about this boy?
Who would people say that he was?

A Different Kind of Doctor

She didn't seem like any doctor the people
had ever seen before. All sorts of people
would come to her. Some of them were rich,
but most of them were poor. They came to
her and asked for help. Sometimes she would
ask them what they wanted; other times she
didn't even have to ask. She seemed to know
even before they said anything. She would
talk to them. Many times she told them to
do something, and then they would get better! People could see the difference right
away. They would look better and act better.
And whenever you asked them about it, they
would say they felt like a new person, not
just on the outside but on the inside, too.

What would people say about this woman?
Who would people say that she was?

From Jeffrey D. Jones, *We Are Baptists: Studies for
Older Elementary Children* (Valley Forge, Pa.: Judson
Press, 2000). Reproduced by permission of the publisher.

The Day the Storm Stopped

The small group of friends was in a boat out on the lake. It was a great day for sailing. It was so pleasant that one of them even fell asleep. But then it started to get dark and cloudy. The wind came up very quickly. Before they could get back to the dock, a horrible storm had begun to rage. Everyone was afraid—everyone except the one friend who had fallen asleep. He kept sleeping. The others couldn't understand how he could sleep when they were so afraid. So they woke him up, shouting, "Don't you care what's happening to us! We might drown!" He just sat there very quietly and said, "Everything is going to be all right." And suddenly the wind died down. The storm was over. The sun even came out again!

What would people say about this person? Who would people say that he was?

Important Bible Words

Caesarea Philippi—a city just north of Galilee that was the seat of government for the region.

prophet—a person who speaks God's word about specific situations or problems, often talking to people about their sins and telling them they should change the way they live. Prophets also often perform miracles.

John the Baptist—a relative of Jesus' who preached about the coming of the Messiah and told people to admit their sins and change their ways to get ready. He had recently been killed by King Herod.

Elijah—a prophet who lived about 850 years before Jesus. He talked about the evil of the king at that time. Many people believed that Elijah would come back to life before God's judgment time to get people ready for the Messiah.

Jeremiah—a prophet who lived about 600 years before Jesus. He talked about the sin of his country and said that God would punish the people by having an enemy defeat them. Even though this made many people angry at Jeremiah, he would not stop, because he believed he was doing what God wanted him to do. He also promised that God would make things right again for the people after their punishment.

Baptists believe in SOUL FREEDOM...

the right and responsibility of each person to decide about Jesus and how to follow him!

Who Do You Say That Jesus Is?

Check the phrases that you would use to answer this question.

_____ a great teacher

_____ a good person

_____ a man who lived a long time ago

_____ my Savior

_____ God's Son

_____ a prophet

_____ my Lord

_____ the Messiah

_____ a miracle worker

_____ a friend to people in need

If Jesus asked me who I thought he was, I would say _____ , because . . .

_____

_____

Message to the Family

This session, "I Decide about Jesus," focuses on soul freedom, the Baptist belief that each person has both the right and the responsibility to determine his or her relationship with God. It encourages children to think about their responsibility to develop their own relationships with Christ.

You can help encourage your child in this by reviewing this material with him or her. Here are some suggestions:

■ Read the three stories and discuss possible reactions of people. The purpose of the stories is to help children think about ways that people in Jesus' day may have responded to him.

■ Talk together about the description of soul freedom that is found in the banner.

■ Read the Bible passage and talk about the important Bible words that are listed in this handout. Discuss why Jesus asked the disciples who they thought he was and what Peter's reply meant.

■ Review the items your child checked in "Who Do You Say That Jesus Is?" Share your own beliefs about Jesus. Encourage your child to talk about the item he or she selected as most important and why.

61

Believers' Baptism
SAYING YES TO JESUS

Bible Basis Acts 8:26–40
Key Bible Verse "What is to prevent me from being baptized?" (Acts 8:36).

A Big Day for Jamal

Jamal was excited. So excited he couldn't sleep any more. He got out of bed and went to the kitchen to get something to eat. Sitting at the table, he began to think about everything that made this day so special.

Today was Sunday and he was going to be baptized. During the morning worship service he and several other people—some of them his age and some of them adults—would take turns going into the water in the tank at the front of the sanctuary. There the pastor would ask them if they believed in Jesus Christ as their Lord and Savior and if they promised to follow Jesus in their lives. Jamal thought about the words the pastor had told him he would say after Jamal answered yes: "I now baptize you in the name of the Father and of the Son and of the Holy Spirit." Then the pastor would dunk him in the water. Jamal hoped that would work out all right. He was worried about going under water, but knew that the pastor had done this many times before so everything should be fine. Even more than this, however, Jamal thought about how wonderful it would be to be baptized. This would let everyone know that Jesus was important to him, that he really believed in Jesus, and that he wanted to live the way Jesus taught us to live. That was what excited Jamal the most.

He'd been going to Sunday school for a long time now. Every year he learned more about God's love for him and how God showed that love through Jesus. This year was different, however. This year his grandmother had died. It was a very sad time for him and his whole family. But even though he was very sad, he also felt God's love in a special way. Knowing God loved him helped him when he was sad. Knowing that God loved his grandmother and that because of that love she was with God made the sadness less difficult to take. The more Jamal thought about this and remembered his grandmother's faith in Jesus, the more he decided that this was his faith, too. He wanted to do something about it. He wanted to say yes to Jesus, too. That was why he had decided to be baptized. That was why today was such a special day for him.

From Jeffrey D. Jones, *We Are Baptists: Studies for Older Elementary Children* (Valley Forge, Pa.: Judson Press, 2000). Reproduced by permission of the publisher.

Acts 8 Crossword Puzzle

Complete each of the sentences, then write the word in the space provided
to complete the crossword puzzle.

1. When people decide to make a commitment to follow Jesus Christ as Lord and
   Savior, they are _____
   in water.

2. A messenger from God is an
   _____.

3. The story of Jesus and what he has done
   for us is often called the _____
   _____ (two words).

4. A prophet of the Old Testament who
   talked about the way God would save
   the people who believed was
   _____.

5. The disciple of Jesus who baptized
   many people and helped the man in
   this story understand more about Jesus
   was _____.

6. The man he baptized was from the
   African country of _____.

7. A small horse drawn wagon with two
   wheels was called a _____.

The Good News about Jesus

Look up the Bible verses that your teacher assigns to you. Write a sentence that describes what these verses tell us about "the Good News about Jesus."

Matthew 5:43–44 _____

_____

Matthew 7:12_____

_____

Matthew 28:18–20 _____

_____

Mark 1:14–15 _____

_____

Mark 9:33–37 _____

_____

Luke 4:18–19 _____

_____

John 3:16 _____

_____

John 10:10 _____

_____

John 11:25–26 _____

_____

John 14:15; 15:12–14 _____

_____

Ways of Saying Yes to Jesus

Check the things you do now. Add any other ways of saying yes to Jesus that you think are important. Then circle one or two that you want to do better.

_____   studying the Bible

_____   praying

_____   helping others in need

_____   forgiving people who treat me badly

_____   treating others the way I want to be treated

_____   giving to the church

_____   loving people who are different from me

_____   being baptized

_____   telling other people about God's love

_____   asking God for forgiveness for the things I do wrong

_____   asking people to forgive me for the things I do wrong to them

_____   going to worship every Sunday

Message to the Family

This session's theme, "Saying Yes to Jesus," focuses on believers' baptism. It helps children to recognize baptism as a way of following Jesus, as well as a promise to follow Jesus in other ways.

You can help encourage your child in this by reviewing this material with him or her. Here are some suggestions:

■ Read the story about Jamal. Talk with your child about why Jamal's grandmother's death would lead to his wanting to be baptized.

■ Read the story about the baptism of the Ethiopian official that is found in Acts 8:26–40. Your child has read and discussed it in class. Ask him or her to tell you what it means.

■ Review the scripture passages in "The Good News about Jesus." Ask your child which ones he or she believes are most important for us.

■ Look at the items in "Ways of Saying Yes to Jesus." Talk with your child about the ones he or she checked and circled.

Handout #3

The Bible
POWER FOOD FOR THE SOUL

Bible Basis 2 Timothy 3:14–17
Key Bible Verse "All Scripture is inspired by God and is useful for teaching the truth, rebuking error, correcting faults, and giving instruction for right living" (2 Timothy 3:16, TEV).

Food for Thought

Lunch time had finally arrived. Curtis couldn't wait to dig his teeth into his tuna fish sandwich. "I'm so hungry," he said to his best friend, Anthony, who always sat with him in the cafeteria. "Did you watch any of that game last night?" he asked between bites. "Unbelievable."

"I missed it," Anthony answered. "I had other things to do."

"Other things to do?" Curtis asked in astonishment. "What could be more important than the big game?" Curtis continued munching as he waited patiently for his friend to answer.

"I was at church," Anthony said.

"Church? On a Wednesday night? What's the deal?"

"We have a weeknight Bible class for kids," Anthony replied.

"That must be an excellent time—not," Curtis said as he unwrapped a piece of chocolate cream pie. "Pretty boring, I'm sure. With all the 'thees' and 'thous,' I can't figure out what's going on in the Bible."

"It isn't like that at all," Anthony explained. "Our pastor makes it interesting. We're studying young people in the Bible. Last night we learned about David. Did you know he was just a kid when God chose him to be king of Israel?"

Curtis dug into his lunch box again and pulled out two apples. "That's cool," he said.

"But what's that got to do with anything that goes on in the twenty-first century?"

"Our pastor says that people in the Bible were just like we are. They had good days and bad days. They messed up sometimes. They acted the same way back then as we do today."

"You go to that Baptist church in town, don't you?" asked Curtis as he opened a bag of chips. "You Baptists are really into the Bible, right?"

"Yes, it's a Baptist church," Anthony said. "Our pastor tells us that we can't really understand who God is and how God wants us to live if we don't read the Bible."

Anthony paused. "Hey, why don't you come with me next week? Maybe then you'll start to see why we think the Bible is so important."

"Now that's food for thought," Curtis said as he swallowed his last bite of lunch. "I'll be there!"

Baptists are faithful
to God's Word!

**Old Testament
Books of the Bible**

Genesis	Ecclesiastes
Exodus	Song of Songs
Leviticus	Isaiah
Numbers	Jeremiah
Deuteronomy	Lamentations
Joshua	Ezekiel
Judges	Daniel
Ruth	Hosea
1 Samuel	Joel
2 Samuel	Amos
1 Kings	Obadiah
2 Kings	Jonah
1 Chronicles	Micah
2 Chronicles	Nahum
Ezra	Habakkuk
Nehemiah	Zephaniah
Esther	Haggai
Job	Zechariah
Psalms	Malachi
Proverbs	

*"All Scripture is inspired by God
and is useful for teaching the
truth, rebuking error, correcting
faults, and giving instruction for
right living" (2 Timothy 3:16).*

Baptists are faithful
to God's Word!

**Old Testament
Books of the Bible**

Genesis	Ecclesiastes
Exodus	Song of Songs
Leviticus	Isaiah
Numbers	Jeremiah
Deuteronomy	Lamentations
Joshua	Ezekiel
Judges	Daniel
Ruth	Hosea
1 Samuel	Joel
2 Samuel	Amos
1 Kings	Obadiah
2 Kings	Jonah
1 Chronicles	Micah
2 Chronicles	Nahum
Ezra	Habakkuk
Nehemiah	Zephaniah
Esther	Haggai
Job	Zechariah
Psalms	Malachi
Proverbs	

*"All Scripture is inspired by God
and is useful for teaching the
truth, rebuking error, correcting
faults, and giving instruction for
right living" (2 Timothy 3:16).*

Baptists are faithful
to God's Word!

**Old Testament
Books of the Bible**

Genesis	Ecclesiastes
Exodus	Song of Songs
Leviticus	Isaiah
Numbers	Jeremiah
Deuteronomy	Lamentations
Joshua	Ezekiel
Judges	Daniel
Ruth	Hosea
1 Samuel	Joel
2 Samuel	Amos
1 Kings	Obadiah
2 Kings	Jonah
1 Chronicles	Micah
2 Chronicles	Nahum
Ezra	Habakkuk
Nehemiah	Zephaniah
Esther	Haggai
Job	Zechariah
Psalms	Malachi
Proverbs	

*"All Scripture is inspired by God
and is useful for teaching the
truth, rebuking error, correcting
faults, and giving instruction for
right living" (2 Timothy 3:16).*

Personalized Bookmarks

Add your own creative touch to complete
and personalize the Bible bookmarks below.
Punch a hole in each one, and then thread
a colorful piece of yarn through the hole.

Give one bookmark to a family member
and one to a friend . . . and keep one for
yourself! Add a personal message to the
two bookmarks you give away—and be
sure to use your own bookmark every day.

Message to the Family

This session's theme, "Power Food for the Soul,"
emphasizes the importance of helping children see
that the Bible is not a book for adults only. The
Bible contains stories and messages that can help
children learn more about God's love for them.

We know your child will want to learn more
about the Bible—and you can help. Three suggestions appear on the following page.

From Jeffrey D. Jones, *We Are Baptists: Studies for
Older Elementary Children* (Valley Forge, Pa.: Judson
Press, 2000). Reproduced by permission of the publisher.

Baptists are faithful to God's Word!

New Testament Books of the Bible

Matthew	1 Timothy
Mark	2 Timothy
Luke	Titus
John	Philemon
Acts	Hebrews
Romans	James
1 Corinthians	1 Peter
2 Corinthians	2 Peter
Galatians	1 John
Ephesians	2 John
Philippians	3 John
Colossians	Jude
1 Thessalonians	Revelation
2 Thessalonians	

"All Scripture is inspired by God and is useful for teaching the truth, rebuking error, correcting faults, and giving instruction for right living" (2 Timothy 3:16).

Baptists are faithful to God's Word!

New Testament Books of the Bible

Matthew, Mark, Luke, John, Acts, Romans, 1 Corinthians, 2 Corinthians, Galatians, Ephesians, Philippians, Colossians, 1 Thessalonians, 2 Thessalonians, 1 Timothy, 2 Timothy, Titus, Philemon, Hebrews, James, 1 Peter, 2 Peter, 1 John, 2 John, 3 John, Jude, Revelation

"All Scripture is inspired by God and is useful for teaching the truth, rebuking error, correcting faults, and giving instruction for right living" (2 Timothy 3:16).

Baptists are faithful to God's Word!

New Testament Books of the Bible

Matthew, Mark, Luke, John, Acts, Romans, 1 Corinthians, 2 Corinthians, Galatians, Ephesians, Philippians, Colossians, 1 Thessalonians, 2 Thessalonians, 1 Timothy, 2 Timothy, Titus, Philemon, Hebrews, James, 1 Peter, 2 Peter, 1 John, 2 John, 3 John, Jude, Revelation

"All Scripture is inspired by God and is useful for teaching the truth, rebuking error, correcting faults, and giving instruction for right living" (2 Timothy 3:16).

Message to the Family (cont.)

■ First, read with your child the story on this handout. Ask your child to name ways in which the Bible is used in your church and home. Ask what its use—or lack of use—suggests about the importance of the Bible in your church and home life. Add your thoughts, as appropriate, so that it does not appear that you are quizzing your child.

■ Second, share with your child a favorite story or passage from the Bible. Explain why this story or passage has particular meaning for you. Then ask if your child has a favorite story or verse he or she would like to share.

■ Third, think with your child about how often your family reads the Bible—and where you place it in your home. Does it sit on a shelf or in a spare room, often unused? Is it displayed in a prominent place so that you think of it often and visitors recognize its importance in your life? Discuss these questions and identify steps you can take to read the Bible more as a family, and place it in a visible location in your home.

Priesthood of All Believers

WE'RE ALL PRIESTS!

Bible Basis Revelation 1:4–6
Key Bible Verse "[Christ] loves us and freed us
from our sins by his blood, and made us to be
a kingdom, priests serving his God and Father . . ."
(Revelation 1:5–6).

You've probably never thought of yourself as a minister before, have you? But guess what? You
don't have to wear a special robe or study at a special school to be a minister. Baptists believe
that a true minister is someone who shows the love of God and Jesus by helping others.

Helping Others

How can you be a minister to others? Read about the hard time some kids have.
Then write about how you can help on the blank lines.

1. Your little brother is afraid of the dark.
   You can help by:

   _____

   _____

2. Your best friend struck out and her team
   lost the game. You can help by:

   _____

   _____

3. One of your classmates is sad because her
   grandfather died. You can help by:

   _____

   _____

When you help others, you are being a minister for God!

And the Bible Says . . .

A special verse in the Bible (Revelation 1:4–6) helps us understand more about what is expected from those who follow God. Write all of the words in the squares marked 1; then continue with the squares marked 2, and then with 3 and 4, to find out what the Bible says.

1 Christ	2 our	3 us	4 priests	1 loves	2 sins	3 to
4 serving	1 us	2 by	3 be	4 his	1 and	2 his
3 a						4 God
1 freed						2 blood
3 kingdom						4 and
1 us						2 and
3 of	4 Father	1 from	2 made			

_____

_____

_____

_____

_____

As one of God's own people, you have been chosen to share God's love with other people.

Reaching Out in Love

Dara was confused. Her Sunday school teacher had told the class that they were all ministers. Dara didn't get it. How could she be a minister? She wasn't an adult. She didn't know all the stories in the Bible. And she was mean to her younger brother. "Me, a minister?" she muttered to herself after class. "Yeah, right!"

Waiting for the school bus the next day, Dara noticed that Rachel, her neighbor, was unusually quiet. She did not seem to be herself. "Why the sad face?" Dara asked. Rachel's eyes welled up with tears. "My baby brother is very sick," she answered. "My mom says he'll have to go to the hospital and have surgery."

Dara looked right at Rachel. "I'm very sorry," she said. "I will pray for your brother, and I will ask the people at my church to pray for him, too." Then Dara gave Rachel a hug. "Let's hope that God makes everything all right," she said.

That night after school, Dara made a bright, colorful card with a rainbow on the front. In big, bold letters, she wrote, "Get well, Stevie." She put the card in an envelope and decorated it with animal stickers. The next morning she put the card in her neighbor's mailbox.

Rachel was not at the bus stop that day or the next. Dara wondered how everything was. Each night when she went to bed, she said a special prayer for Stevie and Rachel. "Please make everything okay, God," she said.

On Friday, Rachel was finally at the bus stop. She came right up to Dara and smiled. "Stevie had the operation," she said, "and the doctor thinks he'll be as good as new. Thanks for your concern and your prayers. You're a terrific friend!"

1. What did Dara do that was helpful to Rachel? _____

_____

2. Have you ever prayed for anyone? When? _____

_____

3. Do you think Dara is God's idea of a minister? Why or why not? _____

_____

Find the Hidden Word

Use the code to color in the spaces and find the hidden word. Then write the word below
to complete a phrase that is important to American Baptists. The code: *1 = blue; 2 = green;
3 = purple; 4 = red*. What color makes the right word to go in the blank spaces below?

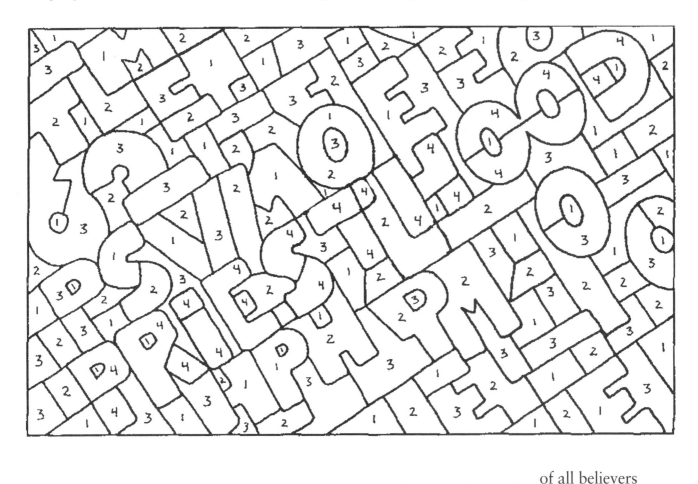

_____ _____ _____ _____ _____ _____ _____ _____ _____ _____ of all believers

This is the phrase Baptists use to describe the biblical message that all Christians are ministers.
So yes, you are a minister!

Message to the Family

This session, "We're All Priests!" explores what
Baptists refer to as the "priesthood of all believers." By this, we mean that all Christians, clergy
and laity alike, are called to love and serve God
and bear witness to Christ.

You can follow up on this session by doing
the following:

■ Review the activities in this handout and
discuss with your child what he or she learned.

■ Read aloud with your child Revelation 1:4–6.
Ask what it means to be one of God's priests.
What responsibilities go with that?

■ Talk with your child about practical ways all
God's people can serve as "ministers" to others
each day.

Religious Liberty
FREE TO BE BAPTISTS!

Bible Basis Acts 5:17–32
Key Bible Verse "We must obey God rather than
any human authority" (Acts 5:29).

Two Days in the Life of Peter

Put an "X" by the items listed below that did not occur in the Bible passage used for
the skits. Then number the remaining items in the order in which they occurred.

_____ The prison guards could not find Peter and the apostles in the jail even though all the
doors were still locked.

_____ Peter baptized those who said they believed in Christ.

_____ An angel freed Peter and the other apostles from jail.

_____ Peter fought with the police who came to arrest him.

_____ The temple police found Peter and the apostles and brought them before the council.

_____ Peter told the council, "We must obey God rather than any human authority."

_____ Peter and the other apostles were arrested for preaching and healing in the temple.

_____ The council demanded that Peter and the apostles explain why they continued to teach
when they had been ordered not to do this any more.

From Jeffrey D. Jones, _We Are Baptists: Studies for Older Elementary Children_ (Valley Forge, Pa.: Judson Press, 2000).
Reproduced by permission of the publisher.

A Pioneer for Liberty— The Story of Roger Williams

He had to keep moving! He knew he must find some kind of shelter from the freezing winds before night came. Roger Williams was still shocked by what had happened to him. He lifted his tired, wet feet through the snowdrift and remembered a night several weeks ago.

"Roger Williams, you must leave as fast as you can!" His friend had hurried to warn him. "The authorities are really angry with you this time! They know you have been talking to people in your home. It was dangerous to preach about religious freedom after they ordered you to leave the colony." His friend was concerned for his safety. "Now they are plotting to kidnap you! They plan to ship you back to England! Escape now!"

Roger Williams fled from the Massachusetts colony. It was winter, 1636. With barely enough to keep him fed and warm, he started the long journey south through the wilderness. While trudging through the snow, perhaps Roger Williams thought about his own life and why he was in trouble. His father had been a merchant in London. This meant that Roger had enjoyed many privileges while growing up. He went to good schools. After his education at Cambridge University, Roger Williams became a minister. "I left England because I think the Church of England is wrong! People have a right to religious freedom," thought Williams. In New England, in the Massachusetts Colony, people soon came to know him as a friendly, outspoken preacher. As pastor of the Salem congregation, he preached boldly about his ideas. Puritan leaders did not like his views.

The Puritans had come to settle in Massachusetts because the Church of England would not change the way they thought it should. They wanted only those people who

agreed with them about religion to live in the colony. The colonial legislature made the laws for the churches. Everybody had to pay taxes to support the churches. There was no choice. Anyone who protested could be expelled.

Roger Williams would not stop speaking out. He said things like: "The government is wrong to make everyone attend church whether they are members or not." "Each person should have a right to choose what to believe." "The church and state should be separate from each other." It did not take long for the government to tell him he must leave the colony. He walked for weeks through the terrible weather. In the spring, Roger Williams bought, from the Indians,

land beyond the Massachusetts border. Together with other followers, he founded Providence, Rhode Island. He saw to it that the charter of the new colony guaranteed full religious freedom to all who came. The risk he took paved the way years later for religious freedom to be included in the Bill of Rights in the Constitution of the United States.

Roger Williams took another stand that was important to Baptists. Soon after he settled Providence, he and several others formed the First Baptist Church in America. He is still honored by Baptists as a person in history who was a courageous pioneer of those ideas for which Baptists stand—religious liberty and separation of church and state.

Adapted from *Baptist Trailblazers* by Arline Ban (Valley Forge, Pa.: Judson Press, 1980).

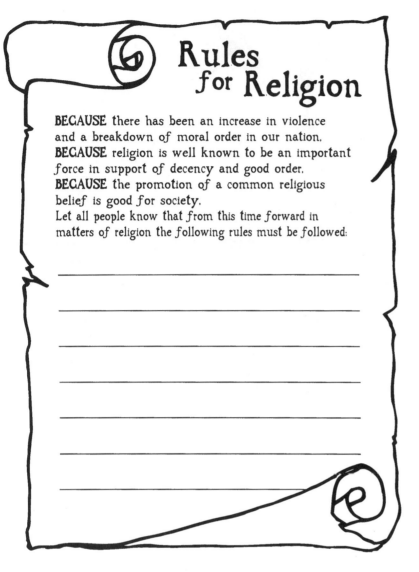

Rules for Religion

BECAUSE there has been an increase in violence and a breakdown of moral order in our nation.
BECAUSE religion is well known to be an important force in support of decency and good order.
BECAUSE the promotion of a common religious belief is good for society.
Let all people know that from this time forward in matters of religion the following rules must be followed:

_____

_____

_____

_____

_____

_____

_____

After you share these rules with others, ask them:

1. How would these rules make your life different?

2. If the government made these rules, do you think you should obey them? Why or why not?

3. Do you think that having separation of church and state in our country protects us from things like this? Why or why not?

Message to the Family

This session's theme, "Free to Be Baptists!", focuses on the importance of religious liberty. It helps children look at the role Baptists have played in ensuring religious liberty.

You can encourage your child's learning by reviewing this material with him or her. Here are some suggestions:

■ Review the story about Peter that the children studied. It is found in Acts 5:17–32. Talk about the courage it must have taken for Peter to tell the authorities he would obey God and not them.

Help your child understand that religious liberty means government is not involved in religion, so we are free to believe and worship as we think we should.

■ Read the story of Roger Williams. Ask your child to talk about why he is such an important person for Baptists.

■ Ask your child to explain the "Rules for Religion" that the class wrote and what they learned from this experience.

Handout #6

Autonomy of the Local Church
IT'S WHAT CHURCHES DO!

Bible Basis Acts 2:40–47
Key Bible Verse "They devoted themselves to the apostles' teaching and fellowship, to the breaking of bread and the prayers" (Acts 2:42).

C
H
U
R
C
H

From Jeffrey D. Jones, *We Are Baptists: Studies for Older Elementary Children* (Valley Forge, Pa.: Judson Press, 2000). Reproduced by permission of the publisher.

Things Churches Do

```
S  P  O  H  I  U  T  R  W  Q  A  O
H  L  E  A  R  N  D  G  J  L  X  R
A  V  P  V  B  N  S  H  A  R  E  H
R  B  R  E  A  K  B  R  E  A  D  Z
E  M  A  F  P  N  V  S  Z  K  H  X
J  F  Y  U  T  E  S  T  I  F  Y  E
E  S  Q  N  I  W  R  E  Y  N  I  G
S  O  Y  P  Z  T  G  A  B  D  G  L
U  W  D  V  E  R  A  C  K  M  A  K
S  T  H  E  L  P  I  H  S  R  O  W
P  I  H  S  W  O  L  L  E  F  H  J
R  E  A  D  T  H  E  B  I  B  L  E
```

_____ worship   share

_____ sing   help

_____ learn   share Jesus

_____ read the Bible

_____ care

_____ have fun

Congregational autonomy is the Baptist belief that every church has the freedom to decide what it will be and do. This includes the freedom to decide how it will worship, how it will organize itself, and what form of ministry it will have. With this freedom comes the great responsibility of listening and following God's will for the church. God is the one who should direct the life and ministry of every church.

Ben's Idea

Ben missed Mrs. Wilson. She used to greet him every Sunday morning and talk to him about things that had happened that week. She always seemed very interested in him and what he was doing. A lot of times he'd even sit next to her in the worship service.

The last few Sundays she hadn't been at church. Ben looked for her every Sunday, but couldn't find her. When he asked his mother where she was, she told him that Mrs. Wilson had been sick and wasn't well enough to come to church. She told him that it might be a long time before Mrs. Wilson could come to church again. Ben wondered if Mrs. Wilson was lonely. He wondered if she missed coming to church. He wanted her to know that he was thinking about her.

In his Sunday school class that morning he talked about Mrs. Wilson. He discovered that the other children all liked Mrs. Wilson, too. She talked to all of them. Together they decided that they should make a card for her.

They drew a picture of a big bunch of flowers on the front. Inside they wrote: "We miss you. Get well soon!" Then everyone signed it.

On the way home from church that day Ben asked his mother to stop at Mrs. Wilson's house. When he went inside she was sitting in a chair in her living room. She didn't look as peppy as she usually did. But when she saw Ben she smiled a big smile. And when Ben gave her the card from his class she was very happy.

Others in the church heard about Ben and his idea. They decided what the class did was a good thing. Then they began to think about other people in the church who couldn't come to church any more. They decided they should do something to let them know everyone at church was still thinking about them and still cared about them. Ben, they said, had helped them discover something new that God wanted them to do.

Message to the Family

The focus of this session, "It's What Churches Do!", is the Baptist principle of congregational autonomy. A brief description of that principle is included in this handout. You can help your child review what she or he learned in the session by doing the following:

■ Read Acts 2:40–47 and then go over the word puzzle. Look for all the words the class found.

■ Look at the description of congregational autonomy. Ask your child to explain this important Baptist concept to you.

■ Read the story. Explore the way in which Ben helped the church find something new that God wanted it to do.

■ Talk about new things God may be wanting your church to do.

Handout #7

Ministry of the Laity
I'VE GOT A GIFT TO SHARE

Bible Basis Ephesians 4:1–7,11–13
Key Bible Verse "... for the work of ministry, for building up the body of Christ ..."
(Ephesians 4:12).

Courtney's Gift

It had been a good day for Courtney. He lay in bed before he went to sleep thinking about everything that had happened.

The day started pretty much the way every day did. There was the struggle to get out of bed and the rush to get ready for school. As usual, he made it to his seat just before the bell rang. It was about midmorning when he began to sense there was something different about this day. It started when the teacher handed back the stories they had written. Everyone got one except Courtney. Just as he was beginning to think that the teacher must have lost his and he'd probably end up getting a failing grade, she told the class there was one story she wanted to read to everyone. It was Courtney's story! After she read it she handed the paper to him. There was a big "A" at the top! Next to the "A" his teacher had written, "You have a real gift for writing, Courtney."

Later during the lunch break a friend was showing Courtney his story. He hadn't gotten a very good grade. As they talked Courtney shared some ideas with her. Together they decided on some changes she could make in the story that would make it much better.

After school was over for the day Courtney went to his church. His Sunday school class had been asked to help in worship the next Sunday. They were getting together to plan

for what to do. Someone needed to give the prayer. Courtney volunteered. While everyone else worked on other parts of the service, he thought about the things he was thankful for, about the people he knew who needed God's help, and about the world and all the things that could make it better. Then he wrote a prayer. When everyone had finished the parts of the service they were working on, his class came back together to share what they had done. When Courtney read his prayer, his teacher and even the kids in his class said it was great.

That night the family had a birthday dinner for Courtney's grandmother. He had been so busy he didn't have time to buy a birthday card for her. So while everyone else was getting the dinner ready he went to his room.

From Jeffrey D. Jones, *We Are Baptists: Studies for Older Elementary Children* (Valley Forge, Pa.: Judson Press, 2000). Reproduced by permission of the publisher.

81

He folded a piece of paper in half and drew a picture on the outside. Inside he wrote a birthday greeting for his grandmother, telling her how much he loved her. When his grandmother opened his card, she was so happy! She said it really meant a lot to her, especially because he had written it himself.

Now as he was lying in bed he thought about what his teacher had written on his story: "You have a real gift for writing, Courtney." He had never thought about it that way before. But the more he thought about it the more he thought that just maybe his teacher was right!

Is This Ministry?

After your class votes on each of these, put a check mark next to
the ones that you think are ministry.

_____   singing in the church choir

_____   collecting food for the food bank

_____   playing the piano

_____   visiting elderly people

_____   bringing a friend to Sunday school

_____   playing on a soccer team

_____   helping a friend with homework

_____   picking up your bedroom

_____   taking your dog for a walk

_____   talking to a friend about something that bothers him or her

_____   saying thank you

_____   praying for someone

Gifts Puzzle

Find and circle all the words that are gifts God gives us.
The words are across, up and down, and diagonal.

F	C	R	E	A	T	I	V	I	T	Y
A	M	Q	N	W	B	E	V	R	C	T
I	X	Y	K	I	N	D	N	E	S	S
T	Z	H	E	A	L	I	N	G	U	I
H	E	L	P	I	N	G	J	L	I	N
K	O	J	P	L	I	F	E	O	H	G
A	G	S	F	D	N	W	Z	R	Y	I
C	A	R	I	N	G	X	T	C	Y	N
V	U	B	I	L	E	A	D	I	N	G

My Gifts and How I Might Use Them

I think some gifts I might have are:

Some of the ways I think I can use these gifts to do God's work are:

Message to the Family

This session's theme, "I've Got a Gift to Share," focuses on the ministry of the laity, the Baptist belief that each person has a gift to be used in doing God's work. It encourages children to discover their gifts and decide how they can be used both in the church and in the world.

You can encourage your child's learning by reviewing this material with him or her. Here are some suggestions:

■ Read "Courtney's Gift" and discuss what his gift was, how he discovered it, and the ways he used it. Talk about what gifts God has given your child.

■ Review the list in the section "Is This Ministry?" Talk with your child about her or his responses and reasons for them.

■ Look at the word puzzle and discuss the gifts that are included in it. It will be especially helpful if you can point out people you know who have some of the gifts that are mentioned.

■ Review the section "My Gifts and How I Might Use Them." Talk with your child about gifts you see in him or her. Discuss ways in which these gifts can be used in God's work.

Discipleship
GROWING UP TO JESUS

Bible Basis Colossians 1:27–29 and Luke 2:41–52
Key Bible Verse "... to bring each one into God's presence as a mature individual in union with Christ" (Colossians 1:28, TEV).

Couldn't and Can

When I was three years old, I couldn't . . .

But now I can!

From Jeffrey D. Jones, *We Are Baptists: Studies for Older Elementary Children* (Valley Forge, Pa.: Judson Press, 2000). Reproduced by permission of the publisher.

God's Secret (from Colossians 1:27)

"God's plan is to make known his secret to his people, this rich and glorious secret which he has for all peoples. And the secret is that . . ."

Jesus Was

Read the following passages from the Bible and decide what they tell us about the ways Jesus was mature. They are all from the Gospel of Luke.

2:41–52

4:1–13

4:16–30

4:42–44

5:27–32

7:11–15

8:22–25

18:15–17

19:1–10

22:39–42

A person who wants to be like Jesus is called a disciple.

More Like Jesus

I want to be more like Jesus by being _____
because . . .

Message to the Family

This session's theme, "Growing Up to Jesus," focuses on discipleship and looks at ways all of us keep growing in our relationship with God. You can help your child review the important things learned in the session doing the following activities.

■ Talk about your memories of your child's learning to do the things that are listed in "Couldn't and Can." Perhaps you can share your own experiences in learning these things as a child.

■ Decode the secret with your child and explore his or her understanding of what it means to have Christ in us.

■ Review the Bible verses and what they tell us about the way Jesus was mature.

■ Explore with your child ways he or she wants to be more like Jesus. Talk about ways you would like to be more like Jesus, too.

Evangelism
I CAN SHARE JESUS WITH OTHERS

Bible Basis Acts 3:1–16
Key Bible Verse "I have no money at all, but I give you what I have: in the name of Jesus Christ of Nazareth, I order you to get up and walk" (Acts 3:6, TEV).

Mary the Evangelist

Mary was shocked. She never knew she was an evangelist. In fact, until that day in Sunday school she didn't even know what an evangelist was.

Mary did know that the church was important to her. She believed in the things she learned there, especially about Jesus. She liked church so much she often invited friends to come with her on Sunday morning and to some of the special events for children, like the roller skating night and the Christmas party. Sometimes she would even tell her friends about Jesus and how much he loved them. It made her feel good to do this because she knew she was talking about something very important with them.

Mary also knew that Jesus wanted her to live a special way. She tried to do that. She tried to care about others, thinking about them first and being kind to them. She was kind to friends and to children who didn't have very many friends. Whenever the church had a special mission project she helped with it. Sometimes it was raising money to give to other people; sometimes it was working in a Christian center to serve meals to people; sometimes it was playing with younger children so their mothers could go to a Bible study at the church.

What Mary learned that Sunday morning was that all of this made her an evangelist! An evangelist is a person who shares Jesus with others. That's what she'd been doing. That's what she had been all along. And she didn't even know it! That's what she decided to keep doing!

A Bible Story about Evangelism

Read Acts 3:1–16. Then use the clues below to fill in the blank spaces.

```
___  E  ___ ___ ___ ___
___  V  ___ ___ ___    ___ ___ ___
___  A  ___ ___
___ ___ ___  N
     G  ___ ___ ___
___  E  ___ ___ ___
     L  ___ ___ ___
___ ___ ___ ___ ___  I  ___ ___ ___
     S  ___ ___ ___ ___ ___
___ ___  M  ___ ___ ___ ___
```

1. The place people went to pray and worship.

2. How often the man was there to beg.

3. What they told the man to do.

4. One of Jesus' disciples.

5. The part of the temple where the man waited for people.

6. Another of Jesus' disciples.

7. The disability the man had.

8. What the people who saw the man were.

9. What the man's feet and ankles became after Peter spoke to him.

10. What the man began doing.

Who are the evangelists in this story? What did they do that made them evangelists?

What Would an Evangelist Do?

You are at a sleep-over at a friend's house. On Sunday morning your parents pick you up to take you to church. Your friends ask you why you have to leave before everyone else. What would an evangelist do?

Your soccer coach calls a practice for Sunday morning during the time your family goes to church. He says everyone has to be there. What would an evangelist do?

In the school yard several children are laughing at a child who limps. What would an evangelist do?

A group of children at your lunch table is making fun of other children who go to church, saying they're just pretending to be good and can't really have any fun. What would an evangelist do?

My Evangelist Checklist

Here's a list of several things an evangelist does. Add others that you can think of. Then check all the ones you think you could do. Finally put an asterisk next to two that you will try hard to do this week.

_____   do nice things for others

_____   help out around the house

_____   talk with my friends about Jesus

_____   invite friends to come to church with me

_____   invite friends to come to Sunday school with me

_____   invite friends to come to other church activities with me

_____   be kind to children who aren't popular at school

_____   help people who are hurt and in need

_____   tell Bible stories to my friends

_____   talk to people about why church is so important to me

Message to the Family

This session, "I Can Share Jesus with Others," is about evangelism. During the session the children have learned that an evangelist is a person who shares Jesus with others and have explored several ways that sharing can take place. They have also been encouraged to think about ways in which they can be evangelists.

You can help your child by reviewing this material with him or her. Here are some suggestions:

■ Read the story "Mary the Evangelist" and talk about why Mary was so surprised to discover that she was an evangelist.

■ Read the Bible story found in Acts 3:1–16 and talk with your child about the ways people in it are evangelists.

■ Go over the word puzzle. Review your child's answers and look at the Bible passage to see where they are located.

■ Look at the incidents described in "What Would an Evangelist Do?" and talk with your child about the skits that were done in class.

■ Review the checklist and discuss the items your child has indicated he or she will try to do in the coming week.

■ Select something that you will do to be an evangelist this week.

■ Your child has been encouraged to pray daily about being an evangelist, so plan a time of prayer with your child each day during the week in which you can focus on how both of you can be evangelists.

Handout #10

Worship
GOING TO A PARTY

Bible Basis Psalm 95:1-7a
Key Bible Verse "O come, let us worship and bow down, let us kneel before the LORD, our Maker!" (Psalm 95:6).

A Party for Karly's Grandmother

When Karly got home from school one day there was a bright pink envelope with her name on it sitting on the kitchen table. She was excited because she didn't get mail very often. She quickly opened the envelope and pulled out the card that was inside. It was decorated with different colored balloons. On the outside in big, fancy letters it said: "It's time to celebrate!" Karly open the card and read the words inside: "You are invited to a party to celebrate the birthday of Esther Smith. It will be held on Friday May 15, 1998 at 7:00 at 222 Belmont Road. Please come!"

Karly knew who Esther Smith was. She was Karly's grandmother! And Karly knew where 222 Belmont Road was. That was her aunt's house. Her aunt was having a birthday party for her grandmother, and she was invited. What fun it would be!

The party was only a week away and there were a lot of things to do. Karly went with her mother to buy a gift for her grandmother. All the time she was thinking that because she loved her grandmother so much she wanted this to be a very special gift. Karly also thought about the special things her grandmother said to her and did with her. It made her happy just to think about those things.

At last the day of the party came. Karly went with her mother and her younger brother, Jason. There were a lot of people there—young people and old people—and they were all having a good time together. Then people began to talk about Karly's grandmother. They told stories about things she had done. People laughed a lot. But some stories made people cry a little bit, too. When they finished the stories, people would talk

From Jeffrey D. Jones, *We Are Baptists: Studies for Older Elementary Children* (Valley Forge, Pa.: Judson Press, 2000). Reproduced by permission of the publisher.

93

about why her grandmother was such a special person. They always said, "Thank you for being so special."

Karly decided she wanted to be part of this celebrating, too. So when it was quiet for a while she told a story about the time her grandmother took her to the zoo and all the fun they had, especially watching the monkeys. Karly told everyone her grandmother was special to her because she always had time to do things with her.

When all the stories were over, Karly's grandmother opened her presents. Then everyone sang "Happy Birthday." Her grandmother cut the birthday cake, and everyone had some to eat. It was a great celebration. It made Karly so happy that for the next week all she had to do was think about it and a smile would come to her face!

Message to the Family

This session, "Going to a Party!", is about worship. It helps children look at the importance of worship in our lives and to consider worship as an important celebration.

You can encourage your child's learning by reviewing this material with him or her. Here are some suggestions:

■ Review the story about Karly and her grandmother. Talk about why the party was so special. Ask your child about the different things people did at the party.

■ Look at Psalm 95. Read it aloud with your child. Ask him or her why this is an invitation to worship. (Verses 1, 2, and 6 offer the invitation. Verses 3–5 and 7 give reasons to respond.)

■ Look over the list that compares the things people did at the party with things that happen in worship. Help your child understand that both are important celebrations.

■ In the weeks ahead, help your child develop a greater appreciation of the importance of worship as celebration by attending worship regularly with him or her. Take the time to point out and explain the various elements of worship that were talked about in this session.

Psalm 95   **An Invitation to a Celebration**

1. Come, let us praise the LORD!
     Let us sing for joy to God, who
          protects us.

2. Let us come before him with thanksgiving
     and sing joyful songs of praise.

3. For the LORD is a mighty God,
     a mighty king over all the gods.

4. He rules over the whole earth,
     from the deepest caves to the
          highest hills.

5. He rules over the sea, which he made;
     the land also, which he himself formed.

6. Come, let us bow down and worship him;
     let us kneel before the Lord,
          our Maker!

7. He is our God;
     we are the people he cares for,
     the flock for which he provides.

When Is Worship Like a Party?

On one side below is a list of all the things that happened at the party for Karly's grandmother. Use the space on the other side to write in things that are mentioned in Psalm 95 and things we do in worship that are like these things.

At the party for Karly's grandmother people . . .

brought gifts

sang songs

told stories about her

shared why they liked her

thanked her for the special things she had done

ate and drank

When we come to worship we . . .

Issues of Faith
SPEAKING GOD'S WORD

Bible Basis Acts 4:23–31
Key Bible Verse "When they had prayed . . . they were all filled with the Holy Spirit and spoke the word of God with boldness" (Acts 4:31).

Peter's Should/Would Story

Peter wondered how it had all happened. It started yesterday. He was on his way to worship at the temple with his friend, John. When he got there he saw a man who could not walk sitting by the main gate. He'd seen him before. He was there almost every day. Because this man couldn't walk, he couldn't work. And because he couldn't work, he didn't earn any money. So every day he would sit by the temple and ask people who were going in to give him some money to live on. Most people felt sorry for the man, so they gave him money. Peter felt sorry for him, too.

But Peter didn't have any money to give him. When he saw the man, he thought, "I may not have money, but I've got something even better. I have faith in a God who has the power to heal people. I'll share that with the man!" And that's what Peter did. He told the man to get up and walk because he was healed in the name of Jesus Christ. Right

---

From Jeffrey D. Jones, *We Are Baptists: Studies for Older Elementary Children* (Valley Forge, Pa.: Judson Press, 2000). Reproduced by permission of the publisher.

away the man began to walk, and all the people who saw him were amazed.

Then Peter began to talk about how this happened. "God loves all of us so much," Peter said, "that God sent Jesus to us to teach us and show us God's love and power. It is the power of Jesus who was raised from the dead after he was crucified that healed this man!"

The people in charge of the temple didn't like what Peter had to say. It was not the faith they had been taught to believe in, and they thought he sounded like he was criticizing them. So they had Peter arrested and

thrown in jail. The next day they made him appear in court and tell his story. They knew they couldn't keep him in jail anymore. But they were still very angry with him and told him never to talk about Jesus again or to do anything like heal in Jesus' name.

Now Peter was free, but what should he do? He believed in Jesus and the power of God's love. But the authorities had told him never to talk about Jesus again.

What would you do?

Read Acts 4:23–31 to discover what Peter did.

Amos's Should/Would Story

Amos lived a long time ago. He lived in the same country Jesus did, but about 750 years before Jesus was born. At that time many people lived well, but other people had very difficult lives. Although the rich lived comfortably, there were many poor people in the county who struggled just to have the food they needed and a decent place to live in. The rich spent their money on expensive jewelry, while the poor didn't have enough to eat. As time went on it seemed that things got worse for the poor, while things just kept getting better for the people who were rich.

Much of the money of the rich people came from cheating other people. They used their wealth to bribe government officials to do what they wanted them to do. And all this time they kept going to the temple to worship God, offering sacrifices to God as they believed good, religious people should.

The more Amos thought about this the more he believed that God wanted him to do something. But what could he do? What could he say? Finally, God's word came to Amos, telling him what to say. What do you think God wanted Amos to say?

To discover some of things Amos actually did say, read the following Bible passages: Amos 4:1–3; Amos 5:11–15,21–24.

Should the church speak about . . .

- fighting in school
- cheating on tests
- children whose families don't have money for food and clothes
- what you'll eat for dinner
- pollution of the air and water

- smoking and drugs
- cleaning up your room
- how much allowance you should get
- how we treat people of different races
- calling other children names

Use the space below to write what you think God wants you to say about one of these issues:

Message to the Family

This session's theme, "Speaking God's Word," focuses on the way in which Baptists take stands on issues of faith. It encourages children to think about what word God wants them to speak on important concerns in their lives and in the world.

You can encourage your child's learning by reviewing this material with him or her. Here are some suggestions:

- Review "Peter's Should/Would Story" and "Amos's Should/Would Story" with your child. Ask the meaning of "should/would." This was used in class as a way to help the children think about what we should do (what God wants us to do) in certain situations and what we are likely really to do. The stories of Peter and Amos were used to explore how two biblical people

said what God wanted them to say even though it was difficult to do so. Talk with your child about the difficulty all of us have at times doing and saying what we think God really wants us to do and say.

- Ask your child to explain what Peter and Amos did.

- Review the list of issues, exploring with your child why he or she believes the church should or shouldn't speak about each one. Then discuss the issue your child decided to write about.

- Follow the example of Peter by praying with your child to ask for boldness in sharing God's love and word with others.

Handout #12

Prophetic Role
BEING GOD'S PEOPLE

Bible Basis 1 Peter 2:1–12
Key Bible Verse "You are a chosen race, a royal priesthood, a holy nation, God's own people, in order that you may proclaim the mighty acts of him who called you out of darkness into his marvelous light" (1 Peter 2:9).

How Do God's People Live?

Fill in the blanks, using the words in italics that describe the way God's chosen people are to live.
   "Be *kind* and *merciful,* and *forgive* others, just as God forgave you because of Christ" (from Ephesians 4:32, CEV).
   "God's Spirit makes us *loving, happy, peaceful, patient,* kind, *good, faithful, gentle,* and *self-controlled*" (Galatians 5:22, CEV).

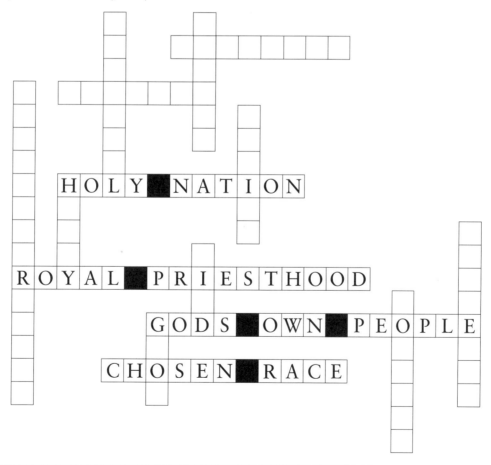

The Chosen Ones

Use the scripts below to develop scenes about the lives of these two Baptists.

Walter Rauschenbusch (1861–1918)

Scene 1: Not quite four, Walter Rauschenbusch winds black crepe on the porch of his Rochester, New York, home the day following the assassination of Abraham Lincoln.

Scene 2: In 1836 Rauschenbusch, a graduate of Rochester Theological Seminary, becomes pastor of a small Baptist church in a poor section of New York City.

Scene 3: Witnessing poverty, malnutrition, and poor living conditions compels Rauschenbusch to work for better living conditions. He sees this as part of his ministry to the people.

Scene 4: Some tell Rauschenbusch this is not a minister's job. He turns to the Bible and finds authority for a gospel ministry that includes social service.

Scene 5: He crusades for playgrounds, parks and decent living conditions. Long hours wear down his health. Sickness leaves him deaf.

Scene 6: Theodore Roosevelt is one of a large number who consult Rauschenbusch on social problems. He continues to work to lessen human suffering at the hands of others.

Scene 7: Through his lecturing and writing, he leads Baptists and other denominations to a renewed sense of the importance of working for social justice.

Scene 8: He teaches for many years at Rochester Theological Seminary. His life is motivated by a desire that God's will be done on earth.

Ann Hasseltine Judson (1789–1826)

Scene 1: In the summer of 1813, a canvas shelter on a rain-swept deck houses Adoniram Judson and his ill wife, Ann, the first American Baptist foreign missionaries, as they journey to Asia.

Scene 2: They reach Rangoon, Burma. Aided by the scholarly Maung Shway-gnong, they begin the study of Burmese from books made from leaves.

Scene 3: A son, Roger, is born in 1815. Within eight months he dies from jungle fever.

Scene 4: The missionaries build a home in Ava. War between Britain and Burma soon begins. Adoniram is jailed on the false charge of spying for Great Britain.

Scene 5: Ann visits the prison with food. She pleads with officials, adopting Burmese dress as a way to show her respect for them.

Scene 6: To save the Burman Bible manuscript on which Adoniram has worked for ten years, Ann sews it inside a mat and sends it to her husband as a pillow.

Scene 7: Adoniram and several other prisoners are removed from their ankle chains and marched to a new jail. With baby Maria and two adopted Burmese girls, Ann follows in a cart. At last the war ends and the Judsons are able to return to Rangoon.

Scene 8: During Adoniram's absence on official business in 1826, Ann's health fails. He returns to a lonely grave on a bluff under a tree.

Debra at School

Debra is in sixth grade. She has been best friends with Becky since before they started school. Becky has become friendly with some other girls and likes to spend time with them. Debra comes across them one afternoon after school. They are in a group standing around Mary, who just moved to town. They've been complaining for some time that Mary "has an attitude" and needs to be put in her place. They have been calling her names and arguing with her. It hasn't gotten physical yet, but it looks like it might. How can Debra act like one of God's chosen people in this situation?

Josh at Home

Things haven't been going well at home lately. It seems like Josh's parents are arguing more and more. He doesn't know why. In fact, it seems like they fight about everything. As Josh is coming home from his friend's one day, he sees his father driving away from the house very fast. When he goes inside his mother is sitting in a chair, crying. Her hair is messed up. Josh thinks she looks afraid. How can Josh act like one of God's chosen people in this situation?

Message to the Family

This session, "Being God's People," focuses on what it means to seek, speak, and act a prophetic word. Acting as God's people is to speak and act God's word for a specific person, time, or place. This is what being a prophet is all about. This material does not use the word *prophet*, rather it encourages children to think about ways in which they can live the special way God wants us to live every day.

You can help encourage your child's learning by reviewing this material with him or her. Here are some suggestions:

■ Review the list of qualities of God's special people that are a part of the word puzzle.

■ Read the stories of Ann Judson and Walter Rauschenbusch and talk with your child about the ways they lived as God's people. Discuss the situations that Debra and Josh found themselves in. Josh's deals with a possibility of physical abuse in a family. This is a difficult topic to talk about. It's important to be open to your child's comments and questions, but it isn't necessary to take the conversation any further than your child leads it.

■ In class the children developed a list of things God's chosen people do. Ask about the things that were on that list and which of them your child believes he or she can do.

Handout #13

Diversity
TOGETHER, EVEN THOUGH WE'RE DIFFERENT

Bible Basis Acts 10:34–35 and Galatians 3:26–29
Key Bible Verse "So there is no difference between Jews and Gentiles, between slaves and free men, between men and women; you are all one in union with Christ Jesus" (Galatians 3:28, TEV).

Peter and Cornelius

Peter was hungry and tired. It seemed like he had been working night and day since that wonderful day when Jesus rose from the dead. So much had happened! After spending time with the disciples, Jesus went back to heaven, telling them it was up to them now. They were the ones who had to share the Good News of God's love with others. And that's what Peter did. He worked hard in the Jewish synagogues telling the story of Jesus. He healed people. It wasn't easy work. More than once he got arrested and put in jail. But he kept at it, traveling all around the country to tell the Good News.

Now he was staying in the home of a friend in a city called Joppa on the coast, about thirty-five miles from Jerusalem. He decided he needed something to eat. While his food was being prepared, he went up on the roof of the house, and a strange thing happened. Peter had a vision. It seemed like a big sheet was coming down out of the sky. In the sheet were a lot of different animals, all of which were animals that the Jewish law said people were not supposed to eat. Then he heard a voice. It said, "Get up, Peter. Kill and eat!" Peter said, "No!" because he knew that

the law didn't allow it. But again the voice said, "Get up, Peter. Kill and eat!" And again Peter said, "No!" But the voice commanded him once more. Then all of a sudden the sheet disappeared, and he was alone on the roof.

While he was wondering what this all meant, visitors arrived at the house. They told him about a vision a man named Cornelius had seen. Cornelius was a Roman soldier, in charge of a group of about 100 soldiers. He lived in Caesarea, which was the Roman headquarters in the country. He was

From Jeffrey D. Jones, *We Are Baptists: Studies for Older Elementary Children* (Valley Forge, Pa.: Judson Press, 2000). Reproduced by permission of the publisher.

a good man, although he was not a Jew. He treated Jews well, but he didn't follow the Jewish laws about what people could and couldn't eat. The visitors told Peter that Cornelius had heard a voice telling him to find Peter and talk to him. When Peter heard this, he made plans to go to Caesarea to meet Cornelius.

When Peter arrived in Caesarea, Cornelius greeted him. He was anxious to hear what Peter had to tell him. Peter began his talk with Cornelius by saying, "I now realize that it is true that God treats everyone on the same basis. Whoever fears him and does what is right is acceptable to him, no matter what race he belongs to." He then went on to tell Cornelius and his family all about Jesus. After they heard what Peter had to say, they decided that they believed in Jesus, too. They were baptized and were some of the very first Christians who did not follow all the Jewish laws about what to eat.

I'm Different!

Find someone in your class who is different from you in each of the following ways. Have them write their names next to the items. You have three minutes.

Color of hair: _____

Favorite food: _____

Month of birthday: _____

Favorite time of year: _____

Color of eyes: _____

Number of brothers and sisters: _____

Color of skin: _____

State you were born in: _____

School you go to: _____

Favorite flavor of ice cream: _____

Famous Baptists

Jesse Bushyhead was a Cherokee Indian who was an important judge of the Cherokee Nation. When the Cherokees were moved from their home in the southern states to Oklahoma in the 1830s, he was one of four Cherokee men who continued to do mission work among their people. He regularly traveled a route that was 240 miles long in order to visit people and churches. He translated some of the Bible into the Cherokee language.

Lulu Fleming was the first African American woman to be appointed a missionary by American Baptists. She went to serve in the Congo in Africa in 1886. When Lulu got sick five years later, she had to come back to the United States. She brought several Congolese youth with her and arranged for their college education. While in the United States, she studied medicine. When she returned to the Congo in 1895 she was a doctor and cared for sick people there. After a few years she got sick again and had to return to the United States. She died in 1899.

Edwin Dalhberg believed in peace. His parents were from Sweden. They moved to the United States and began a church in Minnesota. When Edwin grew up he went to seminary and became pastor of his first church in 1918. During World War II he talked about the importance of peace. This made him unpopular with some people. He was a great preacher and pastor and served as president of the American Baptist Churches. He also wrote books; one was titled *I Pick Up Hitchhikers*. He died at the age of ninety-three.

Concepcion Renteria was sixty-five years old when she became an American Baptist missionary in 1887. But she had already spent many years in mission work in Mexico, her native country. She had no formal training to be a missionary. She didn't go to college or seminary, but she was very successful. She spent many years visiting people in Mexican villages, leading Bible study and preaching. She was so good at this that she became a teacher and taught other people how to be missionaries. She was so excited about sharing the Good News of Jesus that she would even do it with people she sat next to on the train when she was traveling from town to town. She died in 1893.

Orlando Costas was born in Puerto Rico in 1942. When he was twelve, his family moved to the United States. In the 1960s he served as pastor in several churches in New York City. Education was important to him, and so he continued to study even after seminary. He was a professor of a seminary in Latin America. Then he taught at Eastern Baptist Seminary, an American Baptist seminary in Philadelphia. Finally he taught at Andover Newton, an American Baptist seminary near Boston. The most important part of his ministry for him was working with the poor and people who had no power. He believed that this was what Jesus' ministry was about, too. He died at a very early age of stomach cancer.

Isabelle Crawford was known as "the Jesus woman" and "the heroine of Saddle Mountain." She was born in 1865 and served as a missionary for thirty-six years. Most of that time she worked with Native Americans, the Kiowa people in Oklahoma. She brought the Good News of Jesus to them in a place called Saddle Mountain. Isabelle shared the very difficult life of the Kiowa. She stayed with them during famine, when there was very little food to eat. She helped them when promised government help did not come. She believed that many of the difficulties the Kiowa experienced were because of the poor treatment they received from white people. Isabelle shared the gospel with the Kiowa, both in what she said and what she did. She started a school for children, taught sewing, and cared for the sick. Isabelle also worked with Native Americans in Arizona and New York. She died in 1981 at the age of ninety-six.

Lott Carey was born a slave about 1780. He lived a difficult life and did many things that were not good until he became a Christian in 1807. From that time on he devoted his life to telling people about Jesus. In order to do that, he taught himself to read and did whatever he could to learn more about the Bible. Lott got married and had two children. All of this happened while he was still a slave. Finally in 1813 he had saved a total of $850 and bought his and his family's freedom. He continued to share the gospel with others and eventually became a missionary to Africa so that he could share the news of Christ with people in the place his grandmother had been taken from many years before.

Mavis Lee was born in Canton, China, in 1904. By the time she was seventy-seven years old she had earned four different degrees from colleges and seminaries, but she still thought of herself as a learner. She came to the United States in the late 1940s to be trained as a missionary. But communists took over her country and she was unable to return. Her mission field then became the United States. She started a church in California. Later she was a language teacher for the YMCA. She compiled a Chinese and English hymnal. She lived in one of the worst areas of San Francisco, yet because of her love and care for everyone she was respected and loved by all who lived there.

Information on Jesse Bushyhead is adapted from "A Shorter Baptist History in Several Acts" by Warren Mild, *Baptist Leader*, March 1976. Information on other historical figures is from material prepared for Venture, the American Baptist National Youth Gathering in 1994.

Message to the Family

This session's theme, "Together, Even Though We're Not the Same," focuses on diversity. It helps children look at the richness of differences among Baptists, while affirming the unity we share in Christ.

You can help encourage your child's learning by reviewing this material with him or her. Here are some suggestions:

■ Review some of the differences members of the class discovered among themselves.

■ Read the material on important people in Baptist history and talk with your child about the different backgrounds, experiences, and ministries of those people.

Mission

SHARING GOOD NEWS HERE, THERE, AND EVERYWHERE

Bible Basis Acts 1:6–11
Key Bible Verse "You will be my witnesses in Jerusalem, in all Judea and Samaria, and to the ends of the earth" (Acts 1:8).

Jimmy' Story: I Need a Family

"That's it!" Jimmy said to himself. "I can't keep going. My mother didn't care about me. Her friend, who took me in, doesn't care about me. Everything at school is going wrong. I get into fights and the teachers catch me stealing. I'm going to run away!"

And he did. Only eleven years old, Jimmy packed his bag and walked into the woods near Kodiak, Alaska. He lived there many days, all by himself, with only the bag he had packed. Jimmy had run away several times. But finally he said to himself, "Running away isn't solving my problems. I need help."

Jimmy walked out of the woods and found a police station. "Please help me," he said. "There is no one to take care of me. And I can't take care of myself, all alone in the woods."

Some kind people arranged for Jimmy to move to the Jesse Lee Home at Alaska Children's Services in Anchorage. There he would be safe, and the people on staff could help him.

At first, Jimmy couldn't stop worrying about a lot of things — even about where his next meal would come from. He was an unhappy, angry boy with a short temper. But then Jimmy began to change. He learned that he could trust the grown-ups at Alaska Children's Services. And they could see that

Jimmy wanted to make a better life for himself. He began attending church every Sunday and started reading the Bible. "I never felt so good before," he thought.

One Sunday morning, Jimmy bravely stood up in church and told the congregation, "My name is Jimmy. I'm twelve years old and I live at the Jesse Lee Home. I don't have a family, and something I really want in my life is a family. I need your help."

The Smith family heard Jimmy that day. They talked with the staff at the Jesse Lee Home about inviting Jimmy to move into their home. They talked with Jimmy many times. Finally everyone agreed that Jimmy

From Jeffrey D. Jones, *We Are Baptists: Studies for Older Elementary Children* (Valley Forge, Pa.: Judson Press, 2000). Reproduced by permission of the publisher.

would move to the Smiths' home. Mrs. Smith told everyone, "Jimmy is so used to taking care of himself, he does chores without being asked. In fact, we have to tell him to play and not work so hard!"

Today, Jimmy makes A's and B's at school, plays Little League baseball, and enjoys being a Boy Scout. He is grateful for Alaska Children's Services, the people at his church, and for his new family. When Jimmy moved to his new home, he wrote this thank-you note:

"This is for everyone at Jesse Lee Home. Thank you for keeping a roof over my head and keeping me fed. Thank you for helping me through hard times and giving me a hug and for keeping me calm when I was mad. I also thank all of you for being understanding of my situation. Thank you for being a friend."

Sandy's Story: Missionary Body Builder

Sandy Schoeninger is a missionary body builder. She teaches physical education at Kodaikanal International School in South India and coaches intramural track, field hockey, and volleyball teams.

She also directs weekend camping and hiking programs and has won twenty-six hiking awards representing six thousand miles of walking. Those miles have been shared with students and have taken her over much hilly and rugged ground. There's no easy, flat walking here!

"The walks and activities are mission projects, opportunities to witness for Christ and to be a Christian example," Sandy says. "Through our work at the school, these kids are exposed to the gospel of Christ even if they do not make a commitment while they are here."

However, many do commit their lives to Christ at Kodaikanal. God has used Sandy to build bodies that are strong in spirit as well as physically, as she and her students have hiked those six thousand miles.

Witness Unscramble

What does a witness for Jesus Christ do? Unscramble the words below to discover some of them. If you can add others of your own, scramble the letters and see if your classmates can unscramble them.

REAC   __ __ __ __

REEVS   __ __ __ __ __

REHSA EHT   __ __ __ __ __   __ __ __
GDOO SEWN   __ __ __ __   __ __ __ __

VOLE   __ __ __ __

PLEH   __ __ __ __
RESHTO   __ __ __ __ __ __

SSIIMNO   __ __ __ __ __ __ __

ELTL   __ __ __ __
TUOAB   __ __ __ __ __
EUSSJ   __ __ __ __ __

ETIVNI   __ __ __ __ __ __
SDNRFEI   __ __ __ __ __ __ __
OT CCHHUR   __ __   __ __ __ __ __ __

Use this space to write your own words and scramble the letters for others to unscramble.

111

What are the ways you can be a witness for Jesus by sharing good news?
Draw at least one way in the space below.

Message to the Family

This session, "Sharing Good News Here, There, and Everywhere," is about mission at home and around the world. It encourages children to think about what it means to be a witness for Jesus Christ by sharing the good news of God's love for everyone.

You can help encourage your child's learning by reviewing this material with him or her. Here are some suggestions:

■ Review "Jimmy's Story" with your child. Explore the feelings Jimmy might have had at various points in the story. Talk about the people who were there to help Jimmy and how they were witnesses for Christ by sharing the good news of God's love.

■ Look at the "Witness Unscramble" game. If there are words that are not unscrambled, help your child complete them. Encourage your child to think of other things witnesses do, scramble the words, and have you try to unscramble them.

■ Read "Sandy's Story" together. Talk about the things Sandy does that make her a witness.

■ Look at your child's drawing and ask for a description of what he or she does to be a witness for Jesus Christ by sharing the Good News with others.

Baptist Heritage Resources

Brackney, William H. *Baptist Life and Thought: A Source Book.* Revised. Valley Forge, Pa.: Judson Press, 1998.

Uses primary documents from the seventeenth through the twentieth century to provide insight into important Baptist beliefs.

Celebrate Freedom! Macon, Ga.: Smyth and Helwys, 1998.

A Vacation Bible School curriculum based on important Baptist principles.

Gaustad, Edwin S. *Baptist Piety: The Last Will and Testimony of Obadiah Holmes.* Valley Forge, Pa.: Judson Press, 1994.

Written by a seventeenth-century Baptist leader in Rhode Island, this testimony provides revealing details about the roots, schisms, and beliefs of America's first Baptists.

Goodwin, Everett C. *Baptists in the Balance: The Tension between Freedom and Responsibility.* Valley Forge, Pa.: Judson Press, 1997.

A collection of essays, sermons, lectures, and articles that reflect a variety of perspectives on Baptist life in the late twentieth century.

Jones, Jeffrey D. *Keepers of the Faith: Illustrated Biographies from Baptist History.* Valley Forge, Pa.: Judson Press, 1999.

One-page stories of eighty important Baptists told through captioned illustrations. Can be reproduced for use as bulletin inserts or handouts.

Maring, Norman H., and Winthrop S. Hudson. *A Baptist Manual of Polity and Practice.* Revised. Valley Forge, Pa.: Judson Press, 1991.

Draws on New Testament and historical scenes to explore practical implications of the Baptist understanding of the church.

Our American Baptist Heritage. Video series.

A four-part video series on important events and people in American Baptist Life: The First Baptists, Baptists in Early America, Unity and Diversity in the American Baptist Movement, American Baptists Come of Age. Call 1-800-4-JUDSON to order. Valley Forge, Pa.: Board of Educational Ministries, n.d.

People with a Mission. Video.

A video version of a classic filmstrip that tells the story of American Baptists. A script for use with children is also available. Call 1-800-4-JUDSON to order. Valley Forge, Pa.: Board of Educational Ministries, n.d.

Proclaiming the Baptist Vision. Edited by Walter Shurden. Macon, Ga.: Smyth and Helwys, 1993.

Four separate volumes of sermons: *The Bible, The Church, The Priesthood of All Believers, Religious Freedom.*

Shurden, Walter. *The Baptist Identity: Four Fragile Freedoms.* Macon, Ga.: Smyth and Helwys, 1993.

Explores historical origins and contemporary meaning of Bible, soul, religious, and church freedom. Leader's guide available.

Skodlund, John. *The Baptists.* Valley Forge, Pa.: Judson Press, 1967.

A booklet that provides a statement of commonly accepted Baptist doctrines.

Torbet, Robert G. *A History of the Baptists.* 3rd ed. Valley Forge, Pa.: Judson Press, 1963.

A classic and comprehensive history of Baptists.